The Imperial Self

The Imperial Self

An Essay

in American Literary

and Cultural History

Quentin Anderson

Vintage Books

A Division of Random House

New York

Library of Congress Cataloging in Publication Data
Anderson, Quentin, 1912-
    The imperial self.
Includes bibliographical references.
    1. American literature—19th century—History and
criticism. I. Title.
[PS201.A5 1972]   820'.9'003   72-1753
ISBN 0-394-71824-0

Manufactured in the United States of America

First Vintage Books Edition, October 1972

To Martha, Brom, and Max

Preface

When Henry Adams imagined an apocalypse coming about in the 1930's, he thought of it as happening to a society, a collectivity: the extraordinary concretion of human energies around the Virgin in the twelfth century would be followed in the last days by a moment in which the whole community was in the grip of inhuman force. He did not imagine the possibility of a creeping apocalypse brought about by a persisting impulse on the part of individuals to withdraw affect from the collective life.

The historian, chiefly concerned with the behavior of groups, will tend to resist the idea that group behavior has itself lost a measure of its hold over individual imaginations. And it is hard for most people to see how we can become human without each other's help. But an alternate mode of self-validation that openly proclaims its independence of the fostering and authenticating offices of the family and society has persisted in this country since the 1820's, and has exfoliated enormously in the last decade. How widespread has it been? What important variants does it have? What sort of continuity can we posit for it? Questions that have to do with such pervasive and elusive feelings among large groups are the hardest questions in cultural history; an essay such as this can do little more than pose them.

But we are on firmer ground with writers and their audiences. We have been in the habit of calling Emerson, Whitman, and Henry James—the "imperial" selves of my title—representatively American. These three have a profound extrasocial commitment: their imaginative work ignores, elides, or transforms history, politics, heterosexuality, the hope for purposive change. They avoid or omit any acknowledgment that our experience has stubborn and irreducible elements which we cannot in a lifetime either alter or understand. Are these "American" traits in these three?

The conventional answer employs the term "individualism" to categorize these difficult cases, but the individualist is conceived of primarily as an agent, and Emerson, Whitman and Henry James all disavowed the intention to work on us as do politicians, inventors, or merchants. Emerson offers "provocation" rather than instruction, Whitman proposes to work by "indirection," Henry James argues that the maker must sink wholly out of sight in the form, which alone works on us. It is clear that they meant to cast a spell, to alter the color of our consciousness, but this involved a revolution on the inner scene, not action on the outer one. All three believed that the worst thing a man could do was to accept the conditions of action in the society or the community, to pin himself to a particular role.

They carried this further. They denied that identity is fatal, fatal in the sense that we are stuck with the parents we've got, the children we get, the cultural moment in which we find ourselves. The use they found for our uniqueness is not one which launches us on a heroic or even dialectic response to these given conditions; they themselves attempted, and urged us to attempt, to use our sensibilities to incorporate the whole, to take the whole into consciousness. Just what doing this means will take a good many pages to explain.

To provide a contrast with these men, I have chosen Hawthorne rather than Melville, who had a foot in both camps, that of agency and that of incorporation. (Also, his inclusion would have lengthened my essay by half as much again.) Hawthorne was sure that only in society, despite its faults, can we become human, and he took society for granted as the ground of our humanity. In the other three the sanctions provided by human relationships and institutions were shifted within: the self must provide, and this means making new versions of the self (and, in Whitman's case, the body as well).

I believe that the habit scholars have of calling Emerson misty or abstract, calling Whitman a successful charlatan, calling Henry James ambiguous, are but ways of referring to an inchoate perception of the absolutism of the self which is described in this essay. This absolutism involves an extreme passivity, which is complemented by, must be complemented by, the claim of the imperial self to mastery of what has almost overwhelmed it. Emerson's famous description of himself as a "transparent eyeball" is not extravagant; he did on occasion feel himself open to the total flux of being, just as Whitman lay supine and was ravished by "the peace and knowledge that pass all the argument of the earth," and Henry James, whom his brother William called "powerless-feeling Harry," felt that all the things visited upon his small scared consciousness had more of the authority of existence than he. This impulse to a total self-abnegation was countered in all three by the tremendous assertion my title suggests. Anyone who feels himself so subject to the world is open to the fear of invasion and annihilation, the fear that the beast will spring. Hence, Emerson's assertion of self-reliance (a great man fills up the space between God and the mob); hence Whitman's declaration of his power to emit a light beyond light; hence the novelist's assertion in his Prefaces that consciousness is undivided and offers nothing intractable to the artist, and his steady assertion of his moral principle that the only sin is to assume that our divisions of role are absolute; that "consciousness," the total web of experiences and relationships, is split.

If these three were alike in their assertion of an undivided consciousness, can their common disposition be called American? It can if we find a way of relating the needs and impulses of their readers and hearers to their own, and explaining why Emerson's welcome came while he was alive, why Henry James's was deferred for a generation, and Whitman's for almost a century. I have tried to do this.

The attempt involves taking account of shifts in the nature and intensity of psychic needs, the character of investment in our sexual and social roles from generation to generation, something that we are as yet ill-equipped to do. But the immediate urgency and interest of the job is very great because the impulses to disaffiliation, to unliving our bodily and cultural set, are suddenly all around us. This cultural break has antecedents, and this essay is one attempt to point to them. One of the barriers to such an investigation has clearly been the nature of criticism in the epoch recently ended. In that period criticism was at once extraordinarily accomplished and extraordinarily irresponsible in a very simple way: it failed to acknowledge the needs, commitments and values that animated those who wrote it. We need look no further than the critical and scholarly commentary on our three authors to see that their detachment from the ordinary concomitants of growing up, facing up to the plurality of the world, adopting social and sexual roles, is largely ignored. The critics are clearly emotional collaborators.

In the 1950's Lionel Trilling showed that we were taking a more and more detached view of our social ties; he also argued that there was a curious passivity about much of the best work in American literature of the nineteenth century, that it did not make any response to the idea of society as the scene of human action. In *The American Henry James* (1957) I tried to suggest a historical genesis for this attitude in what I called the "hypertrophied self." This attempt to treat Henry James as a figure in the culture whose father had framed his conception of the world met indignant denials. The assertion that James's art yielded a certain *kind* of moral and emotional sustenance suggested that art was not to be examined solely on its own terms. The moment one made a discrimination of kind, art became subject once more to the moral issues of life, and some putative conception of our humanity.

The discrimination suggested that a particular imaginative adventure might enhance or diminish our power to conceive of ourselves and our fellows. This ran counter to the most cherished mystique of the period of the 1950's: that the only thing about our humanity which ought to be admired without qualification is the shaping power of imagination. We were forever implying that art alone liberates; that the conditions of our associated life are always confining or worse. Critics and the scholars who followed them forgot that both have been elaborated by the same animal. We were so busy understanding poetry that we had no time to consider the relation between its makers and their readers, or to try to relate that understanding to the culture in general.

In our very different period—post-modernist, post-new-critical—there are no hedges about the sacred realm of art. Like the formerly sacrosanct plot of green on the university campus, it is now crisscrossed by the paths made by those who are rather frantically seeking to define their humanity, and in the process find art rather more a means than a refuge.

Since my interest is persistently historical, it differs from that of these new seekers. I hope to go on with the historical inquiry. A good deal remains to be done with our nineteenth-century figures if we are to take them seriously as figures in a culture. I have not only neglected

Melville, but Thoreau as well. The latter offers a fascinating contrast with Whitman, whose celebration of his body he clearly opposed, noting at one point that no piece of nature is as alien to him as his own body. He nevertheless claimed quite as much for the self as the other three.

Q A

New City, New York
July 1970

Acknowledgments

I owe thanks to those who read this book in manuscript, Steven Donadio, Lewis Leary, Herbert Leibowitz, Steven Marcus, George Stade, and Lionel Trilling. For useful suggestions and various good offices I wish to thank Emile Capouya, Heyward Ehrlich, Iola S. Haverstick, and Diana Trilling. My research assistant, Dorothy Gregory, ably seconded by Lyndall Gordon, helped me to order the manuscript, and David Webb and others among my graduate students pushed me hard to give a better account of "Crossing Brooklyn Ferry." Columbia University's Council for Research in the Humanities gave me a summer grant for the study of Hawthorne. My most inclusive and long-standing debt is to the members, both past and present, of the English Department in Columbia College, and to the students who have helped them to make it a lively place.

Contents

The Imperial Self

Chapter I

The Failure of the Fathers

My thesis in this book is that the American flight from culture, from the institutions and emotional dispositions of associated life, took on form in the work of Emerson, Whitman, and Henry James, and that it came to a culminating confrontation with what it claimed to supersede—the lives of men and women in society—in the cosmic comedy of *The Golden Bowl*. Hawthorne, the writer committed to society in the English sense, is an essential reference point in the attempt to chart this flight. It was in the great provincial societies, the United States and Russia, that the presumptions on which western society had been built began to die out. In Russia the process was interrupted, if not reversed. But an array of unquestioned beliefs, which in Europe had become subject to dialectical challenge in the course of the nineteenth century, fell silently away in the United States. The conditions of cultural debate did not exist here; no stage on which romantic opposition to a going society, no stage on which the assertion of alienation could be made, was apparent. It was quite as if the primal inquiry on the part of each developing consciousness was shifting from some such question as "What role shall I be given?" to another, "What world am I to possess?" For the first time since Aristotle the habitudes that accompanied the belief that we are social animals were effectively denied on the plane of society itself. This species of questioning, common to ancient gnostics and medieval free spirits, was in itself very old in the west, but the circumstances under which it was renewed were new, and for the first time society was defenseless against them.

The fact that our imaginative desocialization is not a familiar theme in the study of American literature is partly the result of our having attempted to turn all negatives into positives. In this instance, the term "individualism" has substituted for an investigation of the imaginative consequences of an increasing measure of personal isolation, something which followed a lessening of both the density and the stability of the social medium. Individualism, insofar as it stands for the energy, inventiveness, and adaptability of Americans committed to commercial or industrial enterprise, is a name for those personal qualities which foster impersonality in social and economic relations; the individualist is (again, in the very terms of the myth) the man who subjects others to himself through his shrewdness in gauging their appetites or anticipating their needs.

But this particular stereotype is not only inherently suggestive of a diminution of the strength of social bonds; it serves to help us to duck the actual character of our negation of the social bonds as it was imagined in the nineteenth century. Emerson, who is nowadays treated like a national monument and effectively ignored as a figure in cultural history, has to be looked at squarely if we are to understand how the process of shaking off our ties to others was first imagined.

In Emerson, society was not spurned; it was judged irrelevant to human purposes in the measure that it forced or encouraged each of us to assume a distinct role. Transcendentalism, which Emerson described as "the Saturnalia or excess of Faith" [1] in individual powers and individual sufficiency, simply attempted to supplant society. By comparison, romanticism was a laggard, anachronistically involved in its dialectic of self and society, while Emerson and his fellows went forward to explore the meaning of self on the scene constituted by their view of the human state.[2] The hollow ring of studies of American romanticism, or American uses of the gothic convention in the novel, is understandable; these were pasteboard extremities beside the freezing absoluteness of the Emersonian disavowals. The satanic and the angelic are alike meaningless in the light of a consciousness which denies that our sense of ourselves is based on a reciprocal or dramatic or dialectic awareness of one another. In that light bodies no longer touch, the dancer forsakes the dance; it is the *exeunt omnes* of the human play. The effect of Emerson's work may be compared to that sky-sweeping operation Augustine undertook in *The City of God*. Augustine's contemporaries had filled the space between man and God

5

with all sorts of intercessors, benign and malignant; he got rid of them all in order to make man face his God alone. Emerson's faith commanded a more inclusive housecleaning: in the name of his religious impulse he caught up all the roles, human and divine, into the million sundered selves.[3]

In the first half of the last century one had to find a religious sanction for either affirmation or denial of the values of life in society. Perry Miller was right in believing that for the majority the chief affirmation of those values was the revival.[4] For the growing numbers whose prophet Emerson became, religious feeling was ground for denial of what the revival affirmed. The glad tidings which brought you to the mourner's bench were, in Emerson, to be sought within; the personal God was one person too many for the soul which sought its authority in an exploration of its own consciousness.

The very node of shared experience in Emerson's time was religious. Figures as opposed in fundamental ways as Emerson and Hawthorne met, if anywhere, on religious ground. Such evocative commonplaces as the scarlet letter were immediately apprehensible to everybody, though they may look like recondite symbols to us. In religion and not in politics lay the substance of the meaning of associated life. To attack received American belief was to attack religious presumptions, and the rebellious spirits of Emerson's generation struck where the current of human concern ran deep. They were chiefly concerned with transvaluing religious values precisely because the strongest ties binding Americans together were Christian ties. Tocqueville remarked that no one in America had as yet advanced the reason of state as an authority above Christian principle.[5]

Augustine had made a church; Emerson undertook to bring one down—and saw that he would have to take its place. "I said to Alcott that I thought a great man should occupy the whole space between God and the mob," he wrote in his journal for 1836.[6] He quoted Mencius approvingly: his "vast-flowing vigor" was to "fill up the vacancy between heaven and earth."[7] A preliminary statement of his importance is that he transformed or converted religious ideas into something greatly desired by his hearers: he taught the theory and carried on the practice of secular incarnation. He lay behind Whitman's lines

The mechanic's wife with her babe at her nipple
interceding for every person born.[8]

What he did answered to a widespread psychic need in a simple and massive way. This prophet ushered religion underground into the caverns of the self, but all his communicants became sibyls. This effort took him beyond community; it was post-social. During his first voyage to Europe he noted, "We came out to Europe to learn what man can,—what is the uttermost which social man has yet done." The suggestion that Europe is the region of "social man" is significant.[9]

The radicalism of the early Emerson has been diluted for us by his later work, and by interpretations which variously assimilate him to the ethos of isolate entrepreneurs, or to that of an Elbert Hubbard, or to that of Christian Science. One of the most pointed of these dismissals is Santayana's, who saw Emerson as a man who let the formerly religious down easily by using just enough of the vocabulary of religion to reassure his hearers, and not enough to trouble their sleep. In describing the "transcendental philosophy" he wrote that it

> enables a man to renovate all his beliefs, scientific and religious, from the inside, giving them a new status and interpretation as phases of his own experience or imagination; so that he does not seem to himself to reject anything, and yet is bound to nothing except his creative self.[10]

Exquisitely conscious of all the rejections involved—to make them was to become what he called Whitman, a "barbarian"—Santayana could not see the situation of a man who simply finds the fabric of communal life illusory.[11] His Emerson was a refined expression of the popular European view of us as vulgarly optimistic and culturally irresponsible. Santayana was Catholic perhaps only in the measure of his loathing for private judgment, but how very Catholic this made him appear when judging Americans! He missed, as do all such accounts of Emerson, the weight of the job he had taken on, and the force of the demand, both in himself and in his age, that had led him to assume it. Laying all the burdens formerly sustained by religious institutions on the self makes for pain as well as portable moral investments.[12] The course of the last half century, in which Europe too has been engaged in coming out of culture, makes the feat of the "transcendental philosophy" and Emerson in particular seem more momentous, more costly, and altogether irreversible.

The point in stressing Santayana's response to Emerson is that he spoke to his view of the Concord preacher as he might have to his view of Goethe; Emerson, he felt, is to be judged as a figure in a cultural continuum of which he is a part. It is hard to find such judgments in subsequent writers precisely because the large movement of which Emerson is a prophet has deprived them of Santayana's assurance that we are immersed in our culture. I am about to try to suggest why it was both hard and exciting to be Emerson, and why some of his contemporaries wished to emulate him or found him admirable. Explication must look in two directions, but we cannot follow both at once. If we put the emphasis, as I am about to, on Emerson's brave response to a situation of personal and cultural extremity, we must at another moment be prepared to look at the spectacle from the point of view of the abandoned society, from that of the mothers and fathers, children and lovers —even that of supposititious heroes and subjects for tragedy—for all these roles, actual and potential, lost much of their significance for participants in the Emersonian adventure. I have just said that the process turned out to be irreversible, but it is difficult to contemplate even the beginning of the dissolution of society without some shrinking. It was of course only a beginning, and the quite conscious attack upon society itself, rather than upon particular kinds of economic or political organization, is still a relatively new thing.

An impulse to see Emerson as implicated in his period has led some writers to grade him as a failed philosophic idealist. It was admitted on all sides that he hadn't been one, yet there is often in the earlier commentary the implication that in failing to become one he showed a lack of imaginative *élan;* that his insistence on individual moral agency deprived him of the most elegant intellectual option open to his generation. But we are misled if we do not see this rejection as an element in Emerson's power and evidence of his participation in a cultural shift of great importance.

The position Emerson advanced was more tough-minded than that of imported transcendental thought, not less. Since existentialist thought has become common-place, this is much more apparent. Emerson wrote in his journal for 1829 that "all Hume and Germany" made light of individual moral agency, and he meant just what the modern existentialist theologian Berdyaev meant when he wrote, "German idealism sacrificed the soul in the interests of absolute spirit." [13] Emerson was incapable of making distinctions between the position of Kant and those of his successors, but he saw clearly that his own aim was incompatible with a compelling universal reason. This was too high a price to pay for independence from what he and his fellows thought of as the Lockean understanding, the common-sense view that supported institutions and current practice in the state and the churches.

A. Robert Caponigri puts the apparent intellectual consequences of Emerson's position very clearly: "The specific object of intuition, according to Emerson's use of the term, is the realm of spiritual laws; and the attributes which he ascribes to this realm put beyond question its trans-historical character." [14] Disregarding the question of the historical for a moment, I note that what we may call the activity of being Emerson precludes any formulation quite so clear as this. I prefer to say that when the individual seeks sanction for his independent moral vision he "touches base," and the "realm of spiritual laws" is that base. But what the early radical Emerson was excited about was not the existence of the base, but the discovery of the primacy of the individual, who can alone realize the claims of spirit. His most striking statement of the worth of particularity and its relation to universality inverted the emphasis of Caponigri's formulation: "It seems to be true that the more exclusively idiosyncratic a man is, the more general and infinite he is, which, though it may not be a very intelligible expression, means, I hope, something intelligible." [15] This is from the journal for 1830. There is something inclusive that justifies his activity—this is a statement which quickly leads us away from Emerson; *only the activity uniquely mine can manifest the inclusive* —this is a statement which leads us toward an understanding of him.

The beliefs, states of feeling, and activities which grow out of this sentence from Emerson's journal are the ground of everything Emersonian. It is massively simple. Emerson discovered within himself the conviction that to incarnate the whole one must be this particular creature. As a fantasy it is surely related to everyone's wonder over the fact of his uniqueness. Scholarly discussion of Unitarianism participates in the level rationalistic drawl we attribute to Unitarians themselves. We play down the interesting stress it laid on the minds of youngsters who were confronted by the supreme authority of a Jesus who was but a man, and yet had done what a God had long been credited with doing. To a young man with a stronger impulse to believe than we ascribe to most Unitarians, this was momentous indeed. It is plain that Emerson's sentence was a covert reflection on the incarnation, which led him to make an imaginative leap. It is incarnation from the human point of view: the God can be manifest only in that which is a particular, not in generic humanity, not in a second Adam. Our humanity inheres in our distinctiveness. Not, mind you, in our distinctive role vis-à-vis others, who enjoy roles of another kind, but our distinctiveness as against all the rest of humanity. Are we not "only begotten" sons all? As the young man set his observation down, he was not troubled about what would often concern him: How are we to manifest our uniqueness? Idiosyncrasy, he came to see, was mere dumb difference without expressive form. I must come back to the nature and intention of the form Emerson found; I may interject that to find the particular form which would house the universal became the chief business of Thoreau, Whitman, and the Henry James of the "major phase," while in Emerson's case the search for form was, as in Carlyle and Nietzsche, necessarily subordinate to a goal other than that of making.[16]

Emerson's conception of his office was a religious one, and was marked, both in what it carried forward and in what it rejected, by his antecedent Unitarianism. Its beliefs included the attribution of a specific religious sentiment to mankind, inherited from the eighteenth century, and as extrapolated by William Ellery Channing this became the basis of a theory of the atonement as *at-one-ment*, making oneself one with the divine energy and purpose. This was the leading idea of Channing's famous sermon "Likeness to God." Channing, however, clung to a single providence, initiated in time by a revelation, the meaning of which had been illustrated by an exemplary man, Jesus. Emerson dropped the notion of a unique revelation; individuals no longer needed to recapitulate the unique and glorious fulfillment of our humanity, nor to content themselves with a single providence. While Christian history offered but one starting-point, Emerson offered as many as there were men capable of acting on their idiosyncrasies. Yet they must not act as "persons" exerting dominion over the minds of others, for to do so is to reinstitute the evils of historical Christianity. From others we receive "provocation" but not instruction. If grace has been secularized in the communications of individual men, it is clearly not irresistible grace.

In the particular cultural circumstances Emerson's imaginative leap was decisive; he not only said himself, but made it possible for others to say, that the more clearly distinctive the voice of the celebrant, the more unmistakably does he attest the divine in him. Jonathan Edwards was not confronted by such a heresy. Each individual is not simply the originating point of a chain of causation, but becomes the only effectual agency of whatever spiritual powers there may be. The son is not simply the voice of the father; he alone incorporates the universal purpose. The logical flaws in this are apparent, but hardly relevant. What matters is the emotional gain. Emerson did not even think of himself as redisposing the elements of the Christian mythos to a new end, but that is what he in fact did. Nor did he think of himself as depriving the divine father of agency, of weakening the power of all the fathers in the community, but of course he did. What his parents had conferred he too conferred; he married and begot children. But he played another and more exorbitant role as writer and preacher. He became the divine child who eats up the world and then, godlike, restores it as the Word. He moved the task of self-validation within; asserted that the world of generation and action in which his father had begotten him was subordinate to the encounter of the particular and the universal within the self. Our prime business is no longer imagined as either generation or action, but, ultimately, an exhibition of the power of the self to image the world it has incorporated. In the quotation above Emerson speaks of the great man as filling the space between God and the mob. Yet the implication is bolder still. This imagined man has become the only effectual power in human things, greater than priests and kings.

Tocqueville, considering the emotional situation of the citizen of the great democracy, had falsely supposed that the individual would be lost between his sense of his own pettiness and the immensity of the collective colossus, the state.[17] But there was no collective colossus for Emerson's generation. The emotional pressure to which they responded arose out of the fact that there was a vast vacancy where the effective father state had been. That vacancy was filled to some extent by such psychic projections as Emerson's. There is certainly ground for doubting that the state had ever seemed so compelling on this continent as it had in England. A written constitution cannot generate the same kind of allegiance as a king, and the presidents who followed Washington had by no means preserved intact the initial sense of a weight of transferred authority. Yet we persist, I think rightly, in viewing the rise of Jacksonianism as highly important. The shift which took place on the social scene has lately been investigated by David H. Fischer as a transition from a society in which orders of deference were primary to one in which political parties supplanted deference as an ordering principle.[18] However we describe this transition as it affected the society at large, its bearing on our major nineteenth-century writers offers a clue of great importance to their imaginative disposition. The way in which they reckoned with fathers and figures of like authority is central.

In England and America the century was one in which waves of change of every sort were often represented as brought up short before the figure of the father, who, beleaguered but firm, met its challenges in bearded assurance. (Of course, he did not actually assume the beard until the century was half over.) One may suppose that this figure, no more statistically numerous perhaps than in any other time, but widely available as a cultural image to the actual harried persons who were fathers, had been in part created as the power of religious impulse shifted from the older life of settled congregations to the occasional religion characterized by revivals and nurtured in the home.

However the figure of the father gained the distinctive authority popularly attributed to it, it is a striking fact that our nineteenth-century literature was conditioned by the failure of the fathers, the fact that their sons did not accept them as successful in filling the role popularly assigned them. Emerson, Thoreau, Whitman, Hawthorne, Melville, Mark Twain, Henry James—most of the major figures whom we have come to think of as offering a sense of our distinctive qualities were men who had either been let down by their fathers or acted as if they had. I take it to be fact that the authority of the father was not very firmly based in the life of the culture, however widely he was held to be an original source of authority. The stabilities of class and office and occupation were not there to support him, and the pace of change acted, as it has ever since, to lessen the compulsion of the framing demands of his ethos and his politics. When we come upon exceptions among our writers to the rule of the assumed failure of the father, we are startled by the difference in emotional quality. Emily Dickinson, a recluse whose work seems so much more firm, downright—even worldly—than Emerson's, is one such case. That of Henry Adams is more to the immediate point. It almost appears that he is writing in and about a quite different country. It was not that he pronounced his own father a signal success, but that he was deeply sure that the only way one could succeed was to be a father in the wide sense. This conviction is inextricable from Adams's belief that we all stand or fall with the community, and his lifelong concern, in the *History*, the *Education*, the biographies, and his years in Washington, was with effective leadership. Like the sons of James Mill, Thomas Arnold, and Judge Cooper of Cooperstown, he was quite sure that our fate was wholly bound up with the fate of the polity.

Adams, of course, worked in the mainstream of nineteenth-century thought in Europe, which temporalized every belief and institution and ended with Freud's successful attempt to conceive of individuals as the product of a train of interior psychic events which intersected at crucial points the "historical" or interpersonal circumstances of individual lives. To bind the dreamer on the wheel of cause-and-effect was to make him a part of history. Simply by denying a single providence, Emerson stood aside from all this. His contemporary Kierkegaard may serve as a suggestive counter figure, not merely because his thought revolved about his father, but because he gave shape to the dialectical character of individual existence, which Emerson denied. Kierkegaard believed that the unique irruption of the eternal into time was the cause of all we call history; it was the birth of the eventual.

The moment Emerson chose to say that we are not bound by time, that we could all start afresh, was a critical moment in the national consciousness; he appears to have initiated a counterpoint between his strand of the American imagination and temporalized thought of every kind. Had he been another sort of religious thinker he might simply have recapitulated the assertion to be found in Boehme or Swedenborg, that the individual's history parallels the course of a wider providence, and that we can read back and forth from one to the other. Often as Emerson borrowed figures which suggest this familiar parallelism, it is not the main drift of his thought, for it precludes a plurality of providences.

The very use of the term "national consciousness" is probably questionable because the cultural strain Emerson voices may be said to have won out over the possibility of anything "national." American efforts to project a glorious collective life have rung hollow ever since his day. "Young America," "Manifest Destiny," and the imperialist fantasies of the end of the century have, I think, been exaggerated by historians, who find their meat in anything that may be called a "national" impulse. A diffuse sense of the prospect that many people will be successful doesn't amount to a collective dream. It is implausible in the first place that the United States, which seems to have lacked a sense of national direction since the mid-nineteenth century, should have achieved a more than fragmentary view of its future. Our persisting habit of stretching the moral imperatives of individual conduct to cover the aims of the nation-state is an indication of the vacuum that exists in place of a communally shared sense of goal, or indeed of being. Our dreams of empire have had to do with imperial selves. Emerson helped to make the overextension of the significance of individual claims seem a positive value before the middle of the last century. He did so in a double way, advising his fellows to hitch their wagons to a star, and leaving them deliberately in the dark as to whether they might expect to be drawn into a linear or a circular track. Must we always *act* on the conviction that the whole is manifest to our unique selves?

When Emerson told his hearers that they alone could bring about change, and at the same time told them that they were the subjects of an unchanging truth, he was not contradicting himself out of mere willfulness; he was dragging the highly representative problem of being Emerson into the light. Being Emerson involved this very contradiction. We can see why Sherman Paul's careful analysis of the figures in which Emerson tries to marry the terms of the contradiction is so important, although it must be added that that analysis is too much preoccupied with literary form as terminal to tell us what Emerson was up to. The question is, rather, What emotional demand is bending what cultural forms to its uses? The first, the "linear," term of the contradiction implies the necessity of our mediation, our activity; the second does not, since it finds us passive before truth. It is easy to say of the contradiction that it is a case of the generic human inability to wait for certainty. We ordinarily think of this inability as resulting in a harsh and rigid insistence, a proclamation of the complete sufficiency of a conservative (or a madly innovative) stance toward experience. Emerson's response was tough but flexible; he advanced and gave ground, he was conscious of resistance and of his own inconsistency, but he kept offering his view of consciousness and remained assured that it would find a welcome in others, that they would join him on the "platform" he was occupying at the moment. He was forever asserting something about consciousness that we grant readily enough about its early phases. It is imperial to begin with, and only gradually learns to draw boundaries around itself, and to conceive of relations to others as a necessary part of an awareness of the world. But just as Emerson denied that humdrum transcendence we call "history"—the succession of the generations—he denied a history of successive and transcendent changes in the psyche. I quote from "Experience":

Life will be imaged, but cannot be divided nor doubled. Any invasion of its unity would be chaos. The soul is not twin-born but the only begotten, and though revealing itself as a child in time, child in appearance, is of a fatal and universal power, admitting no co-life.[19]

The whole of this essay might be quoted at this point to enforce Emerson's awareness of the difficulties he faced in carrying this undifferentiated consciousness into the arena of adult life. The essay takes us backstage; we see the brilliant analogizing process familiar in *Nature*, "The American Scholar," "The Divinity School Address," "Self-Reliance," going on in the foreground, but it is accompanied by a contrapuntal stress on the resistances offered by experience and the versions of it that Emerson's contemporaries professed, explicitly or tacitly.

It is true that all the muses and love and religion hate these developments, and will find a way to punish the chemist who publishes in the parlor the secrets of the laboratory. And we cannot say too little of our constitutional necessity of seeing things under private aspects, or saturated with our humors. And yet is the God the native of these bleak rocks. That need makes in morals the capital virtue of self-trust. We must hold hard to this poverty, however scandalous, and by more vigorous self-recoveries, after the sallies of action, possess our axis more firmly. The life of truth is cold and so far mournful; but it is not the love of tears, contritions and perturbations. It does not attempt another's work, nor adopt another's facts. It is a main lesson of wisdom to know your own from another's. I have learned that I cannot dispose of other people's facts; but I possess such a key to my own as persuades me, against all their denials, that they also have a key to theirs.[20]

The "child" possessed "of a fatal and universal power" is what Emerson preached despite all the resistances he lists.

To insist that Emerson was a preacher is not to assimilate him to the proponents of the "reasonable religion," Unitarianism. There will be more to say about his relation to that religion further on, but it must first be understood that in emotional intensity, an emotional intensity arising from a contradiction of a finally unresolvable sort, Emerson was more closely akin to his Puritan forebears than to the Unitarians. To take Emerson seriously is to put the contradiction at the center: the attempt to incarnate the universal in the particular was a never-ending struggle which colors everything he did, as did the incommensurability of man and God in Puritan preaching. When we transpose the contradiction into exclusively philosophical or literary terms, Emerson is reduced and attenuated. When we embrace the contradiction as he did, the quantum of emotional energy he brought to his work is felt. He was taking the only step available to him to save what he thought essential in religion. There was no temple for the god save the self. Our awareness that the interiorized God would perish or be transformed is after the fact; for Emerson, the impulse to seat him within overrode everything. By contrast the conventional Unitarian preacher found rationality a sufficient bridge between the everyday world and the divine—there was no contradiction—but for Emerson the struggle within the self was never finished.

Indeed, the essential shift in emphasis may best be understood by comparing the kind of effects Emerson aimed at as preacher with those common to Puritan preachers, who sought both immediate and prospective effects—as did Emerson, but Emerson inverts the order. The Puritan preacher offered the immediate hope of a heart unmistakably moved, a profession socially audible, and demanded conduct of a kind appropriate to saints. The immediate hope was for visible saints. The prospective hope was of an eternity of blissful union with the godhead. Move the god within as Emerson did and the consequence is an inversion. The immediate hope is of a union with the divine, although it can only be fleeting; the prospective hope is of social union, meeting again "on a higher platform," to use Emerson's phrase.

These shifts in the character of the immediate and the prospective involve a sharp diminution in our sense of ourselves as agents whose lives are known through what we do to and with others: the inward scene, the transaction between our vision of the whole and our particular style now incorporates the meaning of those outward doings and sufferings. The outward becomes the mere acting out of the inward.

Yet the world's preoccupations and physical nature, rather than the Bible, afford the material which must be transformed for the uses of the inner stage. We no longer have any need for biblical revelation. In fact, the whole world has become the letter which the imperial self must now interpret. Emerson was freed to sit down before all the conventional concerns of man, a list which the titles of his lectures and essays rehearse, and subdue them to the uses of the spirit. The resistance these topics and modes of seeing the world offered appeared in the language in which they were couched by other men. To appropriate the language of politics or poetry or conventional morality was to set up a tension between the expectations that language gave rise to in Emerson's audience and the voice of the self, which devoted all these terms to the use of the inward empire. It follows that Emerson's prose became the audible or visible vehicle of his struggle to use the particular to manifest the universal. Such a passage as this one from *Nature* repeatedly defeated usage and expectation, appropriating the language to Emerson's ends, although no detached passage can represent the cumulative effect of many such transvaluations of associated terms:

> The problem of restoring to the world original and eternal beauty is solved by the redemption of the soul. The ruin or the blank that we see when we look at nature, is in our own eye. The axis of vision is not coincident with the axis of things, and so they appear not transparent but opaque. The reason why the world lacks unity, and lies broken and in heaps, is because man is disunited with himself. He cannot be a naturalist until he satisfies all the demands of the spirit. Love is as much its demand as perception. Indeed, neither can be perfect without the other. In the uttermost meaning of the words, thought is devout, and devotion is thought. Deep calls unto deep. But in actual life, the marriage is not celebrated.[21]

The daily entry in the journal represents the whole affair in miniature. My idiosyncrasy becomes my way of *taking* the world, my announcement of its union with the universal. "Always the seer is a sayer." But the saying is never conclusive; it acknowledges the mixed character of existence in the very act of invoking totality. The structure of Emerson's writing is in this way like the activity of preaching itself. It has a characteristic wave motion, a series of rising assertions forever beating on the shore of common-sense presumptions about the divided world and the divided self which Emerson's titles for his essays everywhere imply. Emerson could not be accused, as Alcott could, of demanding an immediate and in some sense final leap into the empyrean of "reason." This acknowledgment in the very texture of his prose of our incapacity for a final absorption into being is, of course, the very thing that made him human, apprehensible, and winning to his audiences.

The whole affair would have appeared spiritually licentious to the Puritan preacher: Emerson was forever saying that the appetite for order must be gratified now, can be gratified now, yet to do so in his mixed mode was to represent the difficulties in a way which made him recognizably a preacher, recognizably a man seeking day by day to domesticate a vision. And the texture of the prose operated to conceal the extravagance, the blasphemous character of the appetite itself.

God had been privileged to affect events and to know all that was to be in the same instant. Emerson claimed no more for man than his ancestors had claimed for God, or, more precisely, he claimed that realized human greatness consists in a demand for the immediate realization of our widest vision. This is neither to be omniscient nor omnipotent, but to say that our momentary sensations of omnipotence or omniscience tell us what we ought to become, what state is appropriate to us. In keeping with a widely held assumption that the central matrix of nineteenth-century thought is Hegelian—that all values and beliefs emerged out of history—we may well think Emerson's re-disposition of the divine energies provincial, a little behind the times. Hegel, we often assume, had saved the very conception of God by burying Him in the ongoing life of the community, promising a resurrection and a final self-confrontation with His full reality. But it now seems that the reverse statement would be more accurate if we are seeking to describe the antecedents of the twentieth-century situation: Hegel sought to save the idea of community by burying God in it. Time itself has brought Emerson's terrible clairvoyance into view. The idea of community was dying in him and his fellows. The god could no longer find a temple in the course of national destiny. The explicitness of the terms of the national compact, the explicitness of rational religion, were of course immensely destructive of the energies of belief. To save what they had formerly embodied, one had to act alone. The individual consciousness must shoulder the burden. Secular incarnation, as I have called it, means being one's own redeemer, sitting at God's right hand *and* acting to some purpose in the world. The matter of the remainder of this chapter is those elements of the culture that fostered Emerson's attempt to give form to his contradiction, and the nature of the demands in Emerson himself, and in his ultimately national audience, that his attempts satisfied.

The most obvious cultural antecedents were religious. The sect from which Emerson emerged had made the mediatorial office of Jesus merely exemplary. What he had done all other men must strive to do. In Channing's words,

"God's vicegerent" was "moral principle," which assured us first that we must be virtuous, and second that God would not let us down by contradicting Himself. The reduction of the force of the mediatorial idea had begun long before. The covenant theology itself, by introducing the notion of a body of men associated with God through a compact, had lessened the force of the notion of kingly and priestly and fatherly authority. Emerson wrote of his quirkily Calvinistic aunt, Mary Moody Emerson, that she felt the Christ to be an intrusive figure, a screen between herself and her God. The ground was thoroughly prepared when Emerson announced that the idiosyncratic was itself the mediatorial; that an individual's powers may redirect events and color the whole. In the words of his journal for 1829: "God determines from all the facts, and my earnest desires make one of the facts." [22]

At the time when the future author of "Self-Reliance" was beginning to be sure that his desires counted in the universe, Unitarianism had ruled the roost for some years. Harvard was in its hands; a large proportion of the New England Congregational churches were led by Unitarian pastors, of whom Emerson's father had been one. The intensities of denominational struggle were all to come, if we except the sometimes acrimonious battles fought out in orthodox congregations. But there was a ferment inside the faith, which was officially proclaimed by William Ellery Channing in 1819. It was not originally a question of factions, and hardly became one until Emerson himself, years after leaving the settled ministry, precipitated the dispute over what Andrews Norton called "The Latest Form of

Infidelity" by his address to the theological graduates at Cambridge in 1838.

The ferment looks in retrospect like the consequence of an effort to discover the meaning of a faith so broad and lacking in prescriptions as the one Channing had outlined in 1819. It is best seen in the Unitarian periodical *The Christian Examiner*, which in its liveliest years found a place for much that was new in theology, letters, and social observation. Those whose knowledge of Unitarianism is confined to Emerson's condemnation of its "pale negations" would be astonished by the content of the magazine between 1825, when Channing's major essays began to appear, and the end of the 'thirties. Much of what we think of as Emersonian is commonplace among its more advanced contributors, and this measure of agreement on Emerson's part makes his rejections all the more striking.

He split with his like-minded contemporaries on three crucial questions: the source of religious authority, the importance of society, and the importance of history. Two sentences from Channing's review of Scott's *Buonaparte* in 1828 are representative of the tone and substance of the elder man's position on the first of these questions: "That subjection to the Deity, which, we fear, is too common, in which mind surrenders itself to mere power and will, is anything but virtue. We fear that it is disloyalty to that moral principle, which is ever to be reverenced as God's vicegerent in the rational soul." Channing deplored not only submission to God (or, we may interpolate, the father) but to society: "It is one mark of the progress of society that it brings down the public man and raises the private man." [23] (Jones Very's essay on the epic, later published in the magazine, translates this proposition into the terms of a profound emotional disjunction. It is Very's thesis that in ancient times the source of poetic inspiration was public, and that in his own time it has become exclusively private.[24]) In March of 1829, reviewing a book of extracts from Fénelon, Channing wrote: "If growth be the supreme law and purpose of the mind, then the very truth which was suited to one age, may, if made the limit of future ones, become a positive evil . . ." [25] Together with the assertion of the primacy of inner moral principle, this may be taken as a leitmotiv for the controversy of the next decade among the liberal Unitarians. He reinforced it in a later issue of the same year: "The truth is, and we need to feel it most deeply, that our connexion with society, as it is our greatest aid, so it is our greatest peril." [26] Here society is at once dangerous and indispensable.

In the same year Carlyle, another great secularizer of Christianity, published in the *Edinburgh Review* a sharply contrasting estimate of our implication in the social nexus:

> SOCIETY, the vital articulation of many individuals into a new collective individual, greatly the most important of man's attainments on this earth. . . . Considered well, Society is the standing wonder of our existence; a true region of the Supernatural, as it were a second all-embracing life, wherein our first individual life becomes doubly and trebly alive, and whatever of Infinitude was in us bodies itself forth, and becomes visible and active.[27]

"The infinitude of the private man," which Emerson was some years later to describe as the burden of all his lectures, makes a pretty inversion of Carlyle's position.[28] And Channing had marched a good way toward it. Yet Channing conserved society's reciprocal function; it was somehow involved in the making of men. Both Channing and Carlyle were blithely busy at building new lodgings for religious feeling. Carlyle's enclosed the spiritual possibilities within the body of society; Channing's less clear-cut position gave the preponderant importance to individual perception—an unmediated source of insight implanted by God. In keeping with his general care that no group be given a defining voice for its members, he published an article in which he questioned the multiplication of societies to further various causes, no matter how ostensibly benevolent. Progressive change could not have its origins in these. He had earlier announced very firmly a principle which we recall in Emerson's formulation of it: "We believe that the human mind is akin to that intellectual energy which gave birth to nature, and consequently that it contains within itself the seminal and prolific principles from which nature sprung." [29] This was radical—it meant that the source of change is single men—but Channing persisted in assuming a temporal context, a social and institutional milieu, whereas Emerson simply withdrew the authority of existence from these things: they became phantasmal, mere provisional arrangements. How and why is a puzzling question I will come back to.

Orestes Brownson, like Channing, said in the *Examiner* of these years that old truth has been outgrown and that new institutional forms must be found to answer to the mind's fresh insights. The priority lay with the burgeoning "mind," and in this Frederick Henry Hedge, another contributor, agreed. But of course the priority of the subject meant something rather precise to Hedge, but something much vaguer to Emerson and Brownson, simply because Hedge alone of the group understood Kant's work. He wrote that Kant may be understood only if one is willing to make the effort to recapitulate the deduction of the categories for oneself.[30] The very notion of a *method* of managing the reinforced inner authority was repugnant to Emerson and the other liberal thinkers of the time, as it had been to Emerson's master in this respect, Coleridge. In Andrew Peabody the response to the proclamation of the inward guide was simplistic. "Religion," he wrote, "is not a revelation from without, but an elementary principle of human nature," [31] and George Ripley's agreement took the form of abandoning his pastorate and founding Brook Farm, in which that principle could flower as it would in each member. The impulse on the part of all save Emerson to find the appropriate new social forms did not mean that his contemporaries were not intellectually venturesome. Brownson, for example, turned to speculations about the necessity of a collective salvation and, in a passage reminiscent of Kierkegaard's imagined "man of faith," declared that the real Christians of the moment might be simply unrecognizable to the members of the existent churches.[32] But in both cases society and institutions are involved. When, at the end of the period of the *Examiner*'s flowering, Francis Bowen, a stalwart Lockean, reviewed Emerson's *Nature* (1836), he found it devastating to remark, "A hermitage is no school of morals," [33] and in fact on this point the liberals and conservatives were at one, and Emerson was almost alone.

Time, providence, and society were real for Emerson's contemporaries; they eased the pains of a selfhood so isolated that it might be called antinomian by reference to the compelling needs of the time, and the definition of these needs was carried on in the *Examiner* and elsewhere as part of a discussion of current European works in literature, history, philosophy, and theology. For these men there was a continuing context in which such discussion was not only possible but imperative. The familiar distinction in Emersonian scholarship between Emerson and such "reforming" transcendentalists as Theodore Parker is quite insufficient to describe the importance of this split. Emerson held out against a powerful current of thought: he would not be involved in time, he was not a member of a generation. Almost as if social space had been appropriated as the scene of a designated range of experience, and time by an ultimately Christian view of an hurrying providence, Emerson turned to "nature." His contemporaries, those who were best prepared to sympathize with him, saw institutions as passing but necessary shadows of what welled out of the self; Emerson saw them as fatal to it. In him alone was the social voice stilled in his great years. I do not mean that he had no impulse to find an audience— far from it—but he did not conceive of that audience as needing guidance in framing new institutions, utopian or other.

Emerson's relation to the romantics overseas also involves striking rejections. It is hard to exaggerate the ground-clearing effect of Coleridge, or the enlivening

pleasure of Carlyle's praise. But it is difficult to think of
Emerson as a romantic, partly because of the very differences that set him off from his liberal contemporaries in
this country. The romantics overseas defined the self
within or against society, or urged, as did Wordsworth,
that a proper mode of communal life was essential to their
vision. We may think of Goethe, who also held out against
the time spirit and was committed to a univocal conception
of nature. But he did not encounter a comparable kind of
cultural extremity and he was at the same time an intensely
public figure, whose career was cadenced by successive
achievements and the responses to them. Emerson's audience was not so much created by an artist as found by a
preacher in circumstances of cultural stress Goethe did
not face. The self defined within an envisioned society is
a formula which fits the romancer Hawthorne, and he
may in this way be discussed as a romanticist. But it is in
just this way that Emerson cannot be understood. The
social world was not for him either a home or a significant
and threatening other with which we enjoy a dialectic relation, or in whose denial we affirm ourselves. His sky
was empty of these possibilities; he had to fill it himself.

Did not Emerson's turn to nature mean a significant tie
with Wordsworth? The answer is clearly negative. As so
often happened with Emerson, the difference was expressed in his view of history, both collective and personal.
The "growth" of the poet's mind was an idea which we
may confidently say was quite inapprehensible to Emerson. A genetic account of aspects of the self, a sense of the
various ways in which parents, landscapes, fairy tales, encounters with strangers, are or might be constitutive of our

sense of the world, these things almost make a catalogue of what Emerson could not afford to know without binding himself to human circumstance in a way he would have found crippling. In discussing Goethe in *Representative Men* he let the edge of his scorn show by speaking of those who think "culture" sufficient to make a man. Among commanding American imaginations in his century the number of those who could grant explicit recognition to the role of their parents in bringing them up was very scant. It involves us fatally with generations and with the idea of time to try to reckon with the place of our immediate forebears. This is a question, as my second chapter will show more fully, of a sense of the self based on a sense of our relationships with others, as opposed to an attempt to imagine it as self-begotten. The very idea of parents fractures the univocal consciousness. "Not in time is the race progressive," wrote the Emerson of "Self-Reliance." He was "an endless seeker with no past at my back." And again, "How quickly the old eternity shall swallow up the Time!"

This of course was the voice of the "transcendental" Emerson and not that of his successor and partial continuator, the acute and charming Concord sage, whose struggle with his more assertive younger self was first carefully chronicled by Stephen Whicher.[34] The sequences of his thought often were identical, but the quality of his prose and the quantum of his hopes and fears were often diminished. He was brilliant on Plato, energetic and just on the English or on Montaigne; the prose maintained much of the lordly independence of tone and epigrammatic force of his earlier phase. But he is no longer a figure of great historical importance. The man who for a brief period sustained the tension between idiosyncrasy and universality is our live, our exasperating, and, at the moment, our ignored Emerson. The work of Jonathan Bishop is a happy exception. But in selections from Emerson edited by Mark Van Doren, and by Daniel Aaron and Alfred Kazin jointly, the earlier Emerson has been put in the background. Sherman Paul's book, the best-articulated reading of Emerson ever done, has had something of the same effect. By pressing Emerson's works hard for a paradigm of order ("an astronomy of the imagination") Paul has described a writer not so much contending with a religious problem as resolving an aesthetic one.[35] And this description is achieved at a cost: the tacit denial of what Whicher had established, that is, the fact that Emerson's faith did lessen. Feidelson's attempt to associate Emerson's search for truth with the creation of adequate symbols is highly sensitive and intelligent; his Emerson is a man rehearsing the conditions of a symbolic art he is unable to achieve, which is all very well if one believes that the symbolizing function has a career of its own, but it is meaningless as cultural history.[36] We have only to recall John Jay Chapman's essay on Emerson to face the fact that he was not playing this post-neo-Kantian game; "symbols" are subordinate to the play of the spirit; they are strictly occasional. Hence Chapman, William James, and John Dewey are often better guides to Emerson than literary scholars, tarred though the former are with the particular character of Emerson's own search.[37]

The attempts of the "New Criticism" to isolate and defend the values of art leads one to infer what was not in fact asserted; that these alone were the ark of our humanity—and could remain so only if we disavowed them as the children of our deepest wishes and our sharpest fears. At any rate, the effect of the New Criticism has been to cut art off from the messiness of lives and the incoherence of history. This impulse was strong among those who repossessed Emerson, Thoreau, Hawthorne, Whitman, Melville, and Henry James a generation ago. The end of criticism as it was practiced in the quarterlies during the 1940's and 1950's seems to have been to assure us that our writers were, like the other great ones, secure in achieved form. F. O. Matthiessen's *American Renaissance* was an admirable accomplishment in this kind. Of course, it did contain assertions about the part its subjects played in our nineteenth-century history. We scarcely noted at the time the curious blend of feebleness and violence which attended these historical generalizations; we took quasi-Marxist and populist thought for granted. But no matter how serious this social thought was for Matthiessen and his contemporaries, it is now plain that it was the dying gasp of American criticism's concern with social history. A relatively static and stable society was thereafter silently assumed to exist. Most of the readers of *American Renaissance* quickly learned, in the atmosphere created by the New Criticism, to disregard its social implications. Society and institutions, the feeling-tone of associated life, had ceased to be an ambient atmosphere; history was drying up for those who dealt with our nineteenth-century writers.[38] As I have put it elsewhere, referring to our treatment of our classic writers: "The skin is pulled tight over the realized works of art," or, one might put it, their shape and form tend to be substituted for the American past by literary critics. In the resulting void the suppositions about a governing American myth beat their wings but find scant historical support.[39]

An irony emerges when we consider the likenesses between Emerson's own enterprise and that of the period of the New Criticism: he too was saying that time must have a stop, that society was unthinkable, that history was an insult to the being of our own immediate perceptions—that we were our own fathers. But the fact that Emerson did not limit himself to the attempt to achieve esthetic order, that he did not terminate in form, created a difficulty. Thoreau, Whitman, and Henry James did so, and Emerson seemed mysteriously recreant. We had no way of coping with a preacher. Matthiessen pushed as far as he could the presumption that Emerson's work might be understood through its own internal economy in his analysis of the poem "Days." The choice of this poem is in one respect obviously right, since it deals with a kind of experience which is central for Emerson, and is closely related to the great passage in which he celebrated a triumph over multiplicity. Crossing a bare common dotted with puddles on a winter evening, he was suddenly "glad to the brink of fear." These moments of experience were clearly identical with the "oceanic feeling" Freud has made familiar; they were expressions of a momentary omnipotence—in them the self embraces the world, the world is caught up into the self. But we cannot deny the fact that as clues to the nature of reality such experiences are in the highest degree misleading, great though their momentary authority is. How great those who have had the experience of diminishing to a speck or swelling to an infinite size while falling asleep can testify. Such moments, as Wordsworth knew, are infantile survivals, so wholly subversive of our everyday sense of self that they have an edge of terror, as Emerson noted; he came to the "brink of fear." The ability on the part of a great artist to specify and control such states within a work was a late-nineteenth- and early-twentieth-century discovery, especially notable in Rilke and Kafka. Emerson the poet was wholly incapable of giving formal resolution to them, and the poem "Days" rather referred to than enclosed its matter. Yet the phrase "glad to the brink of fear" is masterly and unforgettable, and to put that phrase to the fore is to come to a general realization: it was in a language striking in the degree of its abstraction that Emerson has his most intimate triumphs over us. Matthiessen's choice is in the end the wrong one. He should have turned to "Brahma," a poem in which Emerson's taste for psychic risk was indulged and anchored by the flat-as-a-pancake conclusion. Even the conclusion is as good as it can be, since there is no way to end an Emerson poem. He lent more credence than talent to his sense that a poem must offer an account at once detached and complete of somebody's spiritual adventure. His own poems—and "Brahma" is the best of them—were neither detached nor complete, and one feels the strain involved in trying to finish the unfinishable.

Jonathan Bishop simply asserts that Emerson's prose is a realized expressive form; that he was primarily an artist.[40] Up to a point this presumption works admirably. Bishop gives us a persuasive account of the sources of the energies of Emerson's prose, a sense of the way in which the characteristic Emersonian accomplishment, the sentence, came into being, how its internal stresses play on one another. And Bishop avoids the refusal of the full Emersonian power common to the recent collections: he asserts that it lies in the early Emerson. But he falls into the idiom of our essentially atemporal age, and writes as if Emerson were an effectual contemporary of ours—"Emerson is a prophet *because* he is an artist"—and calls him the artist of "the very mode of imaginative discovery itself." Further: "He is trying to tell us about the art of experiencing so that we may experience more, and better." Bishop's position is that the Emersonian sentence is not a reflection of a mode of experience; it *is* a mode of experience. This short-circuit so characteristic of the 1950's and early 1960's has the expectable consequence: the Emersonian line is said to descend through, among others, Henry Adams, Frost, and Wallace Stevens, a collocation which rides roughshod over historical distinctions. It is not surprising to find Bishop saying of the "glad to the brink of fear" passage that it suggests "what the romantic has always meant by 'joy' from Wordsworth to Lawrence," a statement so blithely destructive of historical contexts that it surely deserves some sort of prize. The awkwardness of Emerson for us lies in the difference between the meaning of religious assertions and the effect of the sufficiency and finality of art; it is just this difference that Bishop denies.

Coping with what the preacher said means discovering what sort of weight his abstractions bore, what cries, what prayers, what celebrations were being enacted in them. It is a catchword that our nineteenth-century literature was touched everywhere with abstraction. We are right to quote Tocqueville, as we so often do, and he carries us to provisional conclusions. Abstraction is not a merely negative quality, the lack of the power to specify, which one might expect in a new and provincially self-conscious people. As Tocqueville said, it has a positive function: it serves to fill up the space environing the pygmy individuals who collectively compose the enormous nation. But there is more in abstraction than the impulse to sketch arabesques of assertion in the vast. It has historical meaning. Abstraction is not, after all, the quality of Jefferson's prose, or that of the authors of *The Federalist Papers*. Tocqueville wrote as if that prose had not been composed, yet it had, and the qualities of expansiveness and abstraction which came to characterize our diction and locutions in the 1820's were new not in the sense that they were our first response to our newness as a people, or the vastness of our land and expectations: they were new in contrast to the vocabulary of the founding fathers, the tough-mindedness of the tenth Federalist paper, the subtle, aristocratic boldness of Jefferson. The old vocabulary had been established in the pamphlet wars of the Revolutionary period and the constitutional debate; it had been full of harsh distinctions, between mob and ruler, city and town; it had posited rooted oppositions between warring social interests. Like the moribund New England theology, it had offered a set of tropes to represent the recurrent vexations of our limited human condition.

Both in the relatively cultivated northeast and the growing southwest, this dialectic representation of the meaning of human affairs gave way to the expansiveness and abstraction Tocqueville described. We cannot think of this as a response to primal conditions, to the realization of our Adamic state, because a dialectic culture, marked by orders of deference and by more explicit social roles, had after all preceded it. If on the wider public scene it was an age of political parties, of revivalism, of utopianism, and of the growth of associations for benevolent purposes, it was likewise on every man's inner stage an age of revolt against earlier certainties. Erikson's "identity crisis" is a far more appealing model than the Adamic metaphor. In a certain measure we have long accepted this conclusion about the generation of the 1820's. Perhaps I am saying no more than that we have not taken quite literally and naïvely enough the crucial fact that the generation of the founding fathers was gone or going. July 4 took on an apocalyptic finality in 1826, when Jefferson and Adams died on the same day.

In proposing the applicability of Erikson's "identity crisis," one is instituting a frame of reference in which not only the visible issue (a quality called the "Emersonian," for example) but the whole struggle to become a self in the period was involved. What obstacles, threats, characteristic involutions, and transformations were woven into the victory of the accomplished fact? One must rely in part on what does not directly appear, and make inferences from our sense of what is generic in western character structure. We hypostatize a felt connection between individual lives and—in this instance—a diminution (or transformation) of the role of the father in a particular time. In Emerson's case we encounter a definitive transformation of the role. His father's Unitarianism—that of the generation of Buckminster, and of the *Monthly Anthology* group—had undergone important changes by the time Emerson decided that he could no longer hold a post as minister of a parish, but these changes left even the most liberal of the ministers committed to effecting institutional reforms. Moreover, the "reasonable religion" was tied to history by its insistence on a unique revelation and a Christ who though not God was nonetheless "divine." In the hands of Unitarian preachers religion had become very nearly a mere technique, or an empty mythos of rationality. The representative power of the Christian story had altogether vanished. In a world full of death, anomaly, and suffering they preached the benevolence of God and the innate goodness of man. Emerson was very conscious of the falling away from the intensities of the Puritan divines. He did not for a moment credit the arbitrary and angry God, but he could not deny earlier preachers their force. The step he took must be described as an emotional response to the situation he confronted. The universe had been contradictory and uncertain in the account the Puritans gave of it. He moved the contradiction within. God the father ceased to be a person when the son incorporated him. The contradiction ceased to be descriptive of the world at large; it became descriptive of the self. In a word, Emerson took a regressive step in working out the conditions of secular incarnation, but it was at the same time a forward step, for it enabled him to announce man's participation in divinity as not merely analogous but real. Individuals were His only voice on earth. The only authority was within. We all became actors and spectators in our private theater.

We may now come back to the abstract quality of Emerson's prose with more assurance. It is my assumption that his abstractions involved intensities of feeling that are not to be found in the most evocative of his natural references. It is almost comic how often those who write about Emerson refer to the passages in which Emerson himself implored us to deal with immediate particulars. They are forever pouring out "the meal in the firkin, the milk in the pan," [41] and getting what Tantalus got. Emerson was in fact deeply at war on particularity: his weapons were youth, nature, abstraction, the denial of touch, taste, and smell, a timeless classical past—whatever would serve to dissolve objects and our sense of ourselves as defined by our roles. "When the voice of a prophet out of the deeps of antiquity merely echoes to him a sentiment of his infancy, a prayer of his youth, he then pierces to the truth through all the confusion of tradition and the caricature of institutions." [42] Such appeals from the times and from institutions to the resources of the ego often call upon our recollection of the unclouded imperial self of our childhood. He praised lordly boys who judge their elders with clear eyes, and wrote of puberty that it is the passage from "maternal reason to hard, short-sighted Understanding; from unity to disunion . . ." [43] To have the "simplicity of childhood," [44] which frees us of the need to choose, is the goal. We might put it that Emerson's version of Wordsworth's "Ode: Intimations of Immortality from Recollections of Early Childhood" keeps the children sporting on the shore always in view, never comes to the resolution that would close the inner drama, and that it completely fails to specify those elements, like the "Tree, of many, one" that frame and distance experience in such a way that it can be described as successive and susceptible of resolution. In other words, Wordsworth's art would be fatal to the Emersonian sense of the world: it thrusts toward conclusion, and it plants us on a defined scene as in the "Ode," a scene in which the interplay of the mind and the lambs, the senses and the landscape, distances the poem as an object, something that the reader considers in relation to other poems, to what he knows of Wordsworth himself, and so on. In Emerson we never deal with an object in this sense. Nothing weighs upon us as does that turn in the "Ode" when we come upon the Tree—nothing is in that sense a finality, a heavy givenness which we must encounter. Emerson must in this context be but sparingly a poet, or he will destroy his inner drama by making it visibly subject to an outer world, and to the conditions of growth and decay. He must war on particularity because it distracts from the exhibition of the contradiction within.

In this way he was distinct from those writers who shared with him what, in *The American Henry James*, I called "the hypertrophied self." I do not mean to say that the gulf between Emerson's *exhibition* of his struggle to realize the internalized god and their *representation* of such a struggle was absolute. But it is a clear distinction between Emerson and Thoreau, Whitman, Melville (and, as I shall show later) Henry James, who brought the struggle internalized by Emerson to an extraordinary fulfillment by posing against the ideal of an universalized consciousness the plural, acquisitive, heterosexual, role-playing world. It is a curious fact that James Fenimore Cooper, himself a character in that plural world, should have imagined a figure who (in *The Deerslayer*) takes on the overwhelming burdens assumed by the Emersonian self, and makes its claim to a wide dominion over reality. I find it striking that so social a figure as Cooper—a voice from the direction of associated life, befathered, befamilied, and socially classed—was driven to announce that standards could be elaborated and proclaimed by his forest hermaphrodite, a one-man society! But Natty's claim to an extracultural moral authority is of course validated in the field, in warfare, and Cooper saw him rather as an avatar of a new culture than an imperial self who, like Emerson, seeks to encourage others to try for an imperial separateness. The social hope was firmly subordinated in Emerson, for whom heroic action was just one more of the conditioned human states that he tried to reduce to the unconditioned abstractness of the self which creates its world instead of acting in it.

This emphasis on abstractness as a condition of the most vivid exhibition of the internal struggle makes all the more obscure the question of what relation Emerson enjoyed with his audience. How can one communicate the drama of the imperial self? Have not all the roles been swallowed up in the ego? It is tempting to boggle over this: What is the licit and workable method of persuading someone that he all along has incorporated a god? But this is a logical byway at this point. What we must first understand about Emerson's role as preacher is its most commonplace aspect, the kind of effect he shared with every other preacher, despite the fact that he had no defined pastorate. He retained the privilege which all preachers took for granted, that of appealing to his hearers and readers in the name of both immediate spiritual betterment and prospective gains—not, in Emerson's case, in heaven, but in a better world below. Emerson most often, but by no means always, plumped for the receptive mode, because if we act we become involved in a sequence of actions and the immediate significance of our feelings is threatened; our finally effective performance is put off to the coming of some New Jerusalem. To persuade each hearer that in his uniqueness he incorporated the meaning of the whole is what the preacher tried to do. But any attempt to act on this newly won grandeur landed his hearers in the plural world again. The effect on the listener or the reader is a deliberate blurring of the immediate and the prospective. It is the same kind of blurring in both Emerson and the preacher (or, rather, it would be, if we could credit the preacher with Emerson's verbal skill) but, removed from the context of Christian worship, it has a sharply different kind of effect on the hearer. We are now close to the heart of the Emerson mystery, our recurrent wonder about how he really functioned. What is offered as a consummatory experience both for the preacher and his hearers can have no issue in action; its very character as an experience claims so much of the world for the self that it leaves us nothing to act on. We are also in a position to say that most of the confusion about Emerson's philosophy or his performance as a literary artist amounts to blindness to the blurred quality which is the *sine qua non* of exhibiting his inner contradiction. The effect among the members of Emerson's immediately post-Christian audience was stronger than it could have been for a Christian audience.

Emerson's lectures were not doled out week by week in a church. He shared with the revival the quality of being occasional. The burden he laid on his hearers was of course more intense. He appealed to them to create their own Sabbath; he acknowledged that such moments were occasional for him as well. He knew that he was not addressing Margaret Fullers or Jones Verys (of whom he rightly had suspicions). The lecture was all the ritual there was in the lives of many of his hearers; it had to transport speaker and listeners out of their apparent roles; and, as we have just seen, it had to be at once hortatory to immediate ends and final in its effect. It was occasional, but the occasion was always the same. The demand such efforts made on the speaker was heavy. A Webster talking on party issues was snugly ensconced in his role, relied on funded party sentiment, responded to the roars of Whig approval and the hisses of Democrats. But Emerson's audience had left party at the door; it was neither hoop-skirted nor trousered. It was a creation of the age, antinomian man, gathered into the antinomian congregation. Each of its members was expected to be as particular as he could live in order to be as universal as he would. How many understood that in the Emerson of the brave and desperate years—the 'thirties to the early 'forties—the guarantee of their connection with the universal was their existential uniqueness? No doubt many found in Emerson simply a fresh and rather titillating way to be good, to announce their ties to right feeling despite their having discarded a creed. But we have reason to believe that many of Emerson's hearers understood and welcomed the tie between themselves and the nature of things because it answered the same emotional need in them that it fulfilled in Emerson himself: the road to transcendence lay through self-absorption, one had to take possession of the imperium of one's own consciousness.

Yet a good many simple transitive souls who knew more about themselves and their fellows than they knew how to say were puzzled and annoyed; Emerson had borrowed all the terms formerly used to describe relationships instituted by the society and the wider culture for the uses of the inward empire, and the new senses of the words were not always clear.[45] The transitive person, whose world is constituted by his ties with other people, who terminates whether in love or hate or both, in his sense of how it is between him and them, can smell narcissism afar off, and perhaps can get so far as to say that it is always repeating itself, that it is endlessly stitching the web of assertion and beyond belief boring, but all these responses are rather vague. We have only to recall our uncertainties about Henry Agard Wallace to suggest how much plausible goodness can emanate an odor of deep spiritual malaise.

We may also be sure that those who responded to Emerson knew very well they had weekday selves, roles they must play in the parlor, countinghouse, or garden. They simply became sexless and sanctionless, unconstrained by social demands, when considering higher things. Emerson was full of acknowledgments that we must fall back on the commonplace. Transcendentalism is a carefully measured madness, which admits its aberration when ordering coal. It does not sustain; it is occasional like the revival.

Here the objections of an intellectual order present themselves, and it may help to understand Emerson's relation to us if we give vent to them. We have the corpus of

Emerson on our hands—here he is, this great American prophet—and we feel him to be annoyingly occasional, to be downright incomplete.[46] I have noted that this has to do with the fact that he was a preacher, but let's give our impatience rein. Consider the way in which a Blake, a Boehme, a Berdyaev (I take figures widely separated in time, and doctrinally akin to Emerson) grasped his world. He had no weekday consciousness; he found that the husks yielded by sense have a divine use, but he was far from consenting to their weekday authority—all was sabbath with him. How was Emerson related to such thinkers? He was far more bound to his audience. To ask the question is to see how widely and immediately available his work was. He could speak to his fellows without a delay of generations; he was Lowell's "Plotinus-Montaigne." To read Berdyaev after reading Emerson is to feel a great sense of relief. Berdyaev was at war on common sense, on received opinions about the whole meaning of the western tradition, and he had no fear of making his opposition complete, or working it out to its logical consequence. He dealt with our "fall" into objectification. Emerson flirted with the notion; he dealt with history as a dangerous delusion; Emerson denounced it and made covert use of it; he dealt with another "fall" into sexual division, and Emerson, whose whole drift dictates the same conclusion, contented himself with such remarks as "Chastity is perpetual acquaintance with the All," but never made direct war on the emotional meaning of a heterosexual state. Confronted by the full expression of things which got an elided expression in Emerson, one's impatience is reinforced. He was the great lapsed disciple of Boehme and Plato; he was the man who immobilized Swedenborg and borrowed fragments of the arrested vision. But all this instinctive revolt begs the question as to how he functioned with his audience. We may like our ideas finished, but he wanted his work to be immediately effective, he wanted to be carried away and to carry his audience away and to do it again, and then to do it again. A preacher, after all, does not finish preaching.

If this was true of Emerson as a thinker, it was no less true of him as an artist: both powers played second fiddle to the preacher's goals, which coincided with his own emotional needs and those of his audience. Neither thinkers nor artists could have afforded the incantatory inconsequence of this preacher, nor taken, in their own persons, the psychic risks Emerson took to represent the contradiction by which he was ridden. We may return to Wordsworth for an exemplary contrast.

One of the most often used of Emerson's inciting terms was "nature." After the effectual disappearance for him and his self-chosen audience of organized religion, this catch-all term offered the most inviting possibilities for a new conception of experience. The continuities and recurrences of nature offered an imaginative substitute for history. The ostensible subject of Emerson's first book has made comparisons with Wordsworth inevitable, and offered a trap for the unwary. No parallel of consequence is actually observable, because Wordsworth's sense of the uses of "nature" as a unifying term involved a sense of that which lay outside him: nature was a force playing on him, as well as a scene he might modify. Emerson could never lend credence to nature's otherness. His hopes were too high for that. The following passage makes the distinction for us.

> Perhaps after many sad, doubting, idle days, days of happy, honest labor will at last come when a man shall have filled up all the hours from sun to sun with great and equal action, shall lose sight of this sharp individuality which contrasts now so oddly with nature, and, ceasing to regard, shall cease to feel his boundaries, but shall be interfused by nature and shall [so] interfuse nature that the sun shall rise by his will as much as his own hand or foot do now; and his eyes or ears or fingers shall not seem to him the property of a more private will than the sea and the stars, and he shall feel the meaning of the growing tree and the evaporating waters with a more entire and satisfactory intelligence than now attends the activity of his organs of sense.[47]

In Wordsworth,

> *a sense sublime*
> *Of something far more deeply interfused*,

is the sense of something encountered; in Emerson one must fuse with what is perceived, and the difference is crucial. The sensory mode that Wordsworth did not dream of abandoning is to be supplanted. Wordsworth, who went so far as to conceive of the poet as a "Power" among natural powers in *The Prelude*, never, in his most resolutely a-Christian period, would have found it other than deeply confusing to say of him that "the sun shall rise by his will." Wordsworth took great emotional chances, as great poets must, but they remained fundamentally dramatic, a meeting and confrontation of powers within and without. There was no question of the schizophrenic excess of "shall cease to feel his boundaries." That excess was not Emerson's alone in this American period. One of the legends of Davy Crockett, current in the same decade, represented him as setting the sun going after a big freeze, and it is true of our odd little group of comic heroes described by Constance Rourke that they caught up natural powers into themselves. Their loneliness, the lack of attendant figures about them, was Emersonian too. Wordsworth lost both parents early and Emerson lost his father; both men might have been expected to project parents into their work. Wordsworth did;[48] Emerson did not. In him the family constellation falls back into the self. Why? We must conclude that it was through simple necessity, a desperate need to find emotional lodgment in a world shot through with the terror of death.

We are no longer naïve enough to believe that anybody is an optimist by choice, but we have somewhat played down what was apparently compelling for Emerson. In his fourth year his oldest brother, John Clarke, died of tuberculosis, the family scourge. His father had a severe lung hemorrhage when the infant Waldo was five, the year in which his feeble-minded brother, Bulkely, was born. The father died in 1811, the year of the birth of a sister, who lived to the age of three. (The first child of the family, Phebe, had died earlier.) Emerson's own bout with tuberculosis came in his mid-twenties. He lost his beloved wife, Ellen, in 1831, his brother Edward in 1834, and the cherished Charles in 1836—all to tuberculosis. His brother William and his mother survived along with the vegetable Bulkely. These blows, which scholars have been at pains to minimize by reference to the high mortality rates of the period, nonetheless told on Emerson. His counter-assertion, his famous optimism, has been discussed—oh, so seriously!—as his relation to the problem of evil.

I take it that the counter-assertion was dictated by his emotional circumstances. After Charles' death he wrote, "Night rests on all sides on the *facts* of our being, tho', we must own, our upper nature lies always in Day." The death of his much-loved first child, Waldo, in 1842, elicited a very firm denial of the absoluteness of loss, although the poem "Threnody" establishes the force of the actual blow. A paragraph about Mrs. Emerson in Rusk's biography suggests that the "facts" were acknowledged in Concord.

> In his home there was agreement as yet on the grand law of compensation, though experience often seemed to count heavily against it. Lidian, sick and sometimes despondent, still made her "weak & most fearful nature" hold to this faith and so "endure the thought of the evil that is in the world." As late as 1839 she told Elizabeth Peabody, "My Understanding fails to show me how things can be so—yet my Reason when I will listen—steadfastly affirms—All must be for the Best . . . All despondency *is* founded on delusion;—with me, and I think with most, it originates in bodily disease—or fatigue at least—It is in the nerves,—the soul disowns it." Em-

erson, according to Lidian, had no easier time than she in keeping up faith. He was at the very moment, she said, preparing to lecture on human misery. In theory, he made light of it. "But in fact—I scarce ever saw the person upon whom suffering of *others* made so real impression" she added.[49]

It is mistaken to argue that evil ever was or could have been a distinct intellectual issue for Emerson. His fantasy of the imperial self dictated his position. The rather feeble notion of "compensation" would, had Emerson pushed it harder, have proved as reductive as the Unitarian impulse to explain away the contradictions of the Christian mythos.[50] Emerson was always most true to himself when he was making play with his inner contradiction, which was no more finally resolvable than the idea of the trinity. He played with the idea that every evil was in the end compensated for, not because he deeply believed it, but because it offered a defense against the notion that the self could not embrace the world if the world was indeed fatally plural, intractable, and evil. This settled, domestic, responsible man, husband, father, and townsman, devoted the crucial years up to the mid-forties of the century to making public his fantasy of the primacy of the imperial self. When one faces up to the quality of his thought, his endlessly iterative relation to his audience, and his emotional needs, it appears that he made wider and wider claims for the imperial self in those years before the middle forties in proportion to his sense of the "night" all about him rather than in response to a growing "American" optimism. At the very cultural moment when the customary modes of growing up, the customary modes of finding authority and establishing one's relation to it, were rapidly shifting—the Jacksonian era—and the church in which Emerson had been reared was becoming ever more stodgy and superficial, the resident of Concord offered the world the news that God was not dead, but alive in him and all men. It is striking that the most urgent assertion of the address to the Divinity School in 1838 was directed against the abominable notion that God is dead which Emerson detected in the churches. His vehemence tells us what was of moment to him.

Secular incarnation involves a denial of history, membership in a generation, charity, reform, institutional means of every sort, and at the same time an extreme antinomianism, a claim for the supreme authority of the moment of vision. It represents a redisposition of emotional forces in the face of threatening change. It is founded on, but must not be confused with, a regression to the infantile stage in which the world and the self are coterminous. The fruits of the regressions of genius deserve another name. There does not appear to have been a period when Emerson could not function admirably on the plane of the "Understanding." Just before his marriage to Lydia Jackson, in 1835, we find him sweetly, patiently, and laboriously composing a memorial address on the history of the town of Concord!

What I have spoken of as a regression proceeds outward to cultural innovation. Emerson's efforts to unite the fruits of infantile fantasy with adult demands proved extraordinarily successful in the sense that it met matching demands in his audience. How thoroughgoing and inclusive the product of the fantasy was, Sherman Paul has demonstrated—without any acknowledgment of its emotional character—in *Emerson's Angle of Vision*.

To believe oneself the actual focus at which universal and particular intersect is to be a psychotic of the order of Schreber, of whom Freud wrote a study. This distinguished functionary had delusions about "rays" which focused on him while at stool. But to be able to tap these resources of primary narcissism at moments, and to unite them with the experienced flux of day-to-day existence, is to be something quite distinct from a psychotic, even though it sounds very much the same. One of the early letters to Carlyle reports that Emerson is "striving to keep so true a sphericity as to receive the due ray from every point of the concave heaven." [51] The emotional gain of gathering up all the rays of the sun or the father is plain, and it so pervades Emerson that Paul finds it the ordering principle of his imagination.

If Emerson was able to domesticate his sense of the powers of the self among Americans, it is plain that they had an answering need. His private fact became public in his statement of it and their response to it; it was a truth about them and their sense of the world. My supposition, which gains strength from our view of the period of Emerson's intellectual maturation in the 1820's, is that many Americans were more or less unconsciously attempting the emotional task Emerson had undertaken: that of incorporating the powers of the father who no longer seemed to be present, *qua* father, or minister, or state. There came a moment when the loose texture of developing American life made it impossible for many people to credit the authority of those filling these roles. At the outset this drift in the direction of an imperial separateness made itself felt only as a symptom, not a central fact about the lives of masses of Americans. It appeared at roughly the same time as did the reformist and Utopian enterprises of the period, and all these things followed upon the breakdown of the idea of rule by an elite and the election of Jackson. We must be clear about the kind of effect we attribute to Emerson and Emersonianism before 1850: it was a highly important symptom, and what it portended was centrally exhibited later, in industrial America following the Civil War. Our argument for the importance of the symptom in its own time depends not simply on the fact that Emerson found his audience, but also upon the fact that the most masterful imaginations of the period were all affected by it.

The conclusion I have reached about Emerson's listeners and readers is that they wanted what he wanted; the freedom to imagine themselves as possessed of a power literally realizable by no man, and openly fantasied by most people only when they are infants: the power to dispose of the whole felt and imagined world as a woman arranges her skirt. A denial of pain, terror, and death which complements Emerson's own must, as Constance Rourke suggested in describing American comic fantasy on the frontier, have conditioned the exorbitant character of the demands on reality made by some of Emerson's contemporaries. One must crow very loudly indeed to maintain that "our upper nature lies always in Day" if there is no social, institutional support for that claim.

Emerson remarked in his journals and elsewhere that "the Distinction of the new age" [52] was "the refusal of authority." If this was the Emersonian negative, the apparent positive was the demand that we seek out the moment in which the whole is manifest through the grid of our particularity, the moment in which we are "glad to the brink of fear." Emerson's tidings of gladness were not announcements of the nullity of evil, although he sometimes describes them so, but of a conquest, a momentary conquest over the plurality and arbitrariness of existence so complete that the night-time facts are simply wiped out. An emotional constitution such as this, whose triumphs, momentary though they are, had a psychotic completeness, could no more reckon with the dramatically opposed strands in daily experience than it could conceive the funded otherness of sexuality, parenthood, death, or simple heroism. How suddenly remote is the world of *The Federalist Papers*! Reading them, one enters a world in which the life of community is the paramount fact about human beings, and the arrangements to govern it are assumed to have the decisive power to qualify that life. To read Emerson is to find that associated life has become almost unreal, that the middle ground is filled, insofar as it is filled, with projections out of the self. Alongside those who were successfully building canals and winning elections and carrying on the China trade there stood this portent, a young man who denied the meaningfulness of these things as against his inclusive fantasy and got others to listen.

This lapsed preacher's characteristic blurring of the immediate and the prospective became thereafter something built into the American consciousness: the possibility of shifting into the imperial gear, of finding that all public facts, all the old roles, had, even if only for the moment, become mere extensions of private facts; that *res publica* and the glorious explicitness of sexual roles which Hawthorne celebrated at the opening of *The Scarlet Letter* have simply disappeared into the abyss of the single omnivorous consciousness.

Secular incarnation, then, the term with which we began, may be construed as the act not of identifying oneself with the fathers, but of catching up all their powers into the self, asserting that there need be no more generations, no more history, but simply the swelling diapason of the expanding self. It was this inclusive fantasy from which Emerson fell back in later years, but he never found anything satisfactory to take its place, either in the "conduct of life" or any lesser formula. Nor could he take it back. For him, and for us, the failure of the fathers proved definitive.

Millions of actual fathers could and did raise up sons who affirmed their fatherhood by emulating it in their turn. But the imaginative step Emerson had taken was but the first in a series which made his negation of the humdrum transcendentalism of the generations into a seeming positive: the affirmation of the possibility of an imperial separateness and timelessness. The undifferentiated self had been naturalized as a continuing strand in the American imagination.

Chapter II

Hawthorne's Boston

The Hawthorne of the 1940's and 1950's was a distinguished though not finally successful symbolist. He was felt to have tried for the great thing, works realized in form, and very nearly to have succeeded. His accomplishment in form is impressive, but to neglect his preoccupation with the grain of his culture, a complication inevitable in his time, is to distort him badly. I think of him as quite shamelessly concerned about the measure in which his works opened out toward existence and the wide field of events. He didn't weep when he read *The Scarlet Letter* to Sophia because he was touched by the exquisite resonance of the reds and the blacks in his verbal construction, nor simply because he had found an occasion for self-pity: he had written about lovers constrained by a world, by a town, and both the claims of the lovers and the demands of

the town were present and inescapable for him. We seem
not to have noticed how strong his taste for a certain kind
of reality was, how absorbed his awareness of people as
the creatures of a culture was, how shrewd he was about
the quality of contemporary human relationships. The
fables he made have been examined as if they were animated by no more explicit social concern for the 1850's
than we were able to feel about the 1950's. He was a fabu-
list, but the ends to which he fabled were a good deal more
downright, involved him much more directly with the
mess of human circumstance than we admit. It is true that
he sometimes fudged the job; that he was not always
brave, although he was always braver than anyone else;
and it is true that he sometimes accepted too much at the
hands of his culture. But what we have overlooked is an
amazing authority, which in his own age was his alone.
"Her deepest voice lacks a response; the deeper her cry, the
more dead his silence." [1] This sentence about Zenobia in
The Blithedale Romance carries with it a whole set of implications: that life is rootedly reciprocal, that people are
known through their relationships to other people, and
that the fantasies we try to enact, the aspirations we express, the religious convictions we uphold, are to be
praised or dispraised on the ground that they foster or im-
poverish our relationships with those around us. There are
other things about Hawthorne we have failed to emphasize: that the most hated child in American fiction was
also the first child, that her mother was the first woman,
that is, the kind of creature who if not complemented by a
man will not (*pace* Emerson and Whitman) really become a full-fledged person. Hawthorne saw human selves

as fostered in a net of relations, finding their meaning and value only through those relations. This is a thumping commonplace or an almost heroic achievement, depending on what you love and what moves you.

If we find it hard to account for the way Hawthorne moves us, if what lies beyond the symbolic resonance of reds and blacks is difficult to enunciate, it is not because critical fashion has temporarily obscured our understanding, or not for that reason alone; it is because the future for which Emerson spoke has been realized: our view of persons has rather more to do with their symbolic representations of themselves than with their ties to others. The exploitation of the self has proceeded in step with the exploitation of the continent. The conception of society as a reciprocal affair for which Hawthorne spoke now seems English or European. In his own time it was already receding so fast that he had to invent fables to stand for its settled conditions, conditions a George Eliot could assume. He had to build his own Boston, the town which he made the scene of *The Scarlet Letter*. We recognize our depleted awareness of ourselves as reciprocally conditioned when we take pleasure in the fibrous density of the nineteenth-century novel in Europe or England. But of course we are hardly prepared to find an analogous pleasure in Hawthorne, whose name is a byword for isolation. We might recall that he made it so himself, and we may infer that he believed there was something to be isolated from, despite the assurances of Emerson and Whitman that there wasn't.

We may nonetheless be sure that Hawthorne would find it strange that his exploration of both the necessity and the cost of community in *The Scarlet Letter*, so largely couched in symbol and paradigm, should now seem the most effective his age managed. But it does, and we cannot doubt that Hawthorne hoped that it would have this kind of effect. Our problem is that for the decades just past Hawthorne's own deepest concern has become subliterary. Since it was elided or ignored by Poe, Melville, and Henry James, and actively subverted by Emerson and Whitman, we have the further excuse that it seems almost un-American. The fact that Hawthorne was, to put it in our Emersonian way, horizontally obsessed, that he recorded the adventures of the self only to bring it before a social bar, has become almost unintelligible to us; criticism does not have a vocabulary to deal with this aspect of his work. He has suffered heavily from the disappearance of what Denis Donoghue calls the "ordinary universe," [2] suffered in proportion to his larger stake in it. When criticism lost its power to deal with the public world, and the novel was thought to have lost much of what Malcolm Bradbury is reduced to naming its "referential" [3] dimension, the power of *The Scarlet Letter* became invisible to critical eyes.

In part what we must recapture is "our" Hawthorne, as Lionel Trilling's essay on Hawthorne and his critics suggests—the Hawthorne who was an "American" fact for Henry James.[4] But we have to go further than James did or could; we must grant actuality to what James in 1879 found almost imperceptible, the grain of American communal existence. Professor Trilling puts this more generally. Speaking of the fact that Hawthorne's art refused to catch up and judge all existence, to shut us up to a great "tyrant-dream," as does Blake's, he writes:

And in the degree that he does not dominate us, Hawthorne cannot wholly gratify us, moderns that we are. He is an exquisite artist, yet he suggests to us the limitations of art, and thus points to the stubborn core of actuality that is not to be overcome, and seems to say that the transaction between it and us is after all an unmediated one.[5]

That hidden presumption of the epoch of criticism now ended—where history was, let art now be—is almost completely self-defeating in the case of Hawthorne, who from solitude and secrecy is always to be observed struggling toward the warmth of felt human presences. The inversion of the imaginative direction of Emerson and Whitman is striking: Hawthorne paid his community the tribute of more belief than it could perhaps reasonably invite, while the former two busied themselves with an imaginative undoing of such communal ties as they felt.

No one now seems to take seriously Hawthorne's concern for the quality of life in his society, but there is a recent book in which his own emotional commitments are investigated, Frederick Crews's *The Sins of the Fathers.*[6] This clever book shows Hawthorne humped over his ever-intensifying Oedipal difficulties, attacking fathers, splitting the fatally attractive mother into a darkly sexual figure and a fair, fostering Phoebe, succumbing in the end to "a death-struggle against the conscious emergence of patricidal and incestuous thoughts."[7] Our response to Hawthorne is a response to his compelling use of these primal motifs, and he is finally describable as an "obsessed writer."[8] Crews's dissection of certain stories, particularly

Rappacini's Garden and *Roger Malvin's Burial*, is very useful. Where Hawthorne goes wrong, through over-determination or the intrusion of unmastered material, Crews goes right. But our most general impression is that Crews has examined the wound and overlooked the bow, or its uses, to twist Edmund Wilson's title.

It will help to explain the cultural situation in which Hawthorne's work now stands if we pay some further attention to Crews, who seems quite distinct from the analysts of Hawthorne's reds and blacks, because he asserts that there was a man called Hawthorne, who was in an agonizing fix. That that fix had any relation to Hawthorne's own time, that there were modes of expressing it in his time, that Hawthorne made a triumphant use of those modes, extended those modes, to exhibit the qualities of his own time, Crews does not acknowledge. We may put it down as axiomatic: if Hawthorne had great powers as a writer, they must be thought of as powers to make a particular use of the available spectrum of customs and attitudes, the available translations of primal impulse into social and literary conventions. His use of these things, his imaginative reworking of them, his emphases, his render-ings, his very distortions, are of these things made avail-able to him by his age. (I include of course the way in which the texts of Bunyan and Spenser bore on him and the way in which he responded to them.) His society—to name things both Crews and I believe central for him—offered views of, attitudes toward, marriage, manhood, womanhood, parenthood, and it is what happens to such views in Hawthorne's work that we must consider, are in-deed considering, when we read him. I am restating the commonplace that a great writer becomes exemplary by offering a compelling image of his own time, and that only those writers who have done so can enter powerfully into another time. To make Hawthorne exemplary on the grounds available in our time is to make him the victim of a temporally determined version of the Oedipus complex, and is even more obscurantist than the efforts of symbolist critics to put him and others in a timeless heaven of art.

Hawthorne saw society in *The Scarlet Letter* and *The Blithedale Romance* as the scene on which the qualities and energies of manhood and womanhood were deployed. He had at hand not simply an ample quantity of unresolved Oedipal emotion, but a cultural expression offered by the society as to the character of manhood and womanhood. Cancel out his employment of these and you get case history at the expense of history. Readers of Augustine's *Confessions* would, if they followed Crews, report that it was merely a book by Monica's son, and that the Catholic church—mother church—was merely Oedipal happenstance, the creation of an obsessed theologian.

Consider Crews's treatment of one of the greatest of Hawthorne stories, *Young Goodman Brown*. "His forest journey, in fact, amounts to a vicarious and lurid sexual adventure," says Crews.[9] He shows that the story establishes the sexual guilt of the father, who is said to have participated in an orgiastic witches' sabbath, and that Brown is led to assume a classically split view of his wife, as both madonna and whore. But the story as a story turns out to have a merely illustrative significance. He explains that whether or not "Brown's forest adventure was real or dreamed . . . we cannot quite dismiss his attitude as un-

founded. . . . The only sure point is that by indulging
these fantasies Brown *has* become different; at least one
case of human foul-heartedness has been amply docu-
mented, and for all we know, Salem may be teeming with
latent Goodman Browns." [10] There is both historical na-
ïveté and immediate misreading here. The astonishing
remark about the possible plurality of young Goodman
Browns in Salem means that Hawthorne cannot be given
credit for the fidelity of his story to its dramatic and—at
the time it was written—widely apprehensible Christian
premise. The point of the ending is of course that Salem
sees Brown as probably damned because *he* altogether
lacks charity. The notion is about as familiar as that of
Burns's "Address to the Unco Guid or the Godly Right-
eous," and the turn Hawthorne has provided is simply to
make Brown feel that they are all damned together. The
opposed fictional supposition, the cost to a whole town of
its self-righteousness, is of course amply demonstrated in
The Scarlet Letter. Brown casts out the population of
Salem just as Boston casts out Hester. To say in the context of the story that Salem may be teeming with Young
Goodman Browns is to say that the structure of the story
exists to be seen through, and that that more antique version of our relation to the father called Christianity (more
antique than this rigid Freudianism) is wholly irrelevant
to the species that made it. That Brown is represented as
obsessed, that his tacit proclamation of the universality of
sin is itself the greatest sin and a betrayal of faith, an implicit assault on the deity, is obvious too, but it sounds less
modern than the Oedipus complex. Do we have to spell it

out that Salem wasn't as gloomy as Brown because Salem, for the purposes of this story, hadn't lost its faith?

In approaching *The Scarlet Letter*, the weight of Christian presumption in *Young Goodman Brown* needs to be noted. When we subtract it the story becomes a puzzle. But the striking thing about *The Scarlet Letter* is a change in this narrative mode. If Hawthorne found support in propositions actually or ostensibly Christian in the stories, he shifted his ground in *The Scarlet Letter:* its judgments are based largely on considerations generated within the work itself; it accounts for its own sternness; it has an air of demonstration. Hester's punishment is to Dimmesdale's suffering as public infamy is to private shame. This of course is the principal and most variously played upon of a multiplying series of curious proportions that are not proportions. We may call them paradigms. For example, Pearl is to Hester as Dimmesdale's priestly office is to him; both are bound to the town, although in different ways. Again, Hester's crime is to the town as the minister's is to Chillingworth. These juxtapositions multiply wherever we look. The greater the measure of Dimmesdale's self-accusation, the greater the conviction of his holiness on the part of the town. Or, to quote a characteristic instance of this schematic aspect of the fictional structure, which comes from the climactic scene in the wood, "Here, seen only by his eyes, the scarlet letter need not burn into the bosom of the fallen woman! Here, seen only by her eyes, Arthur Dimmesdale, false to God and man, might be, for one moment, true!" We are aware that these opposed and contrasting terms are in any strict sense ways of relating incommensurables; Hawthorne has none of Spinoza's conviction that he can make an actual geometry of the passions. We are also aware that the first thirteen chapters are on the whole dominated by this species of static tension expressed in what I have called paradigms, sometimes spelled out, sometimes implied, but steadily building an effect of energies playing in ways viewed as exemplary.[11] The mode of the stories has been left behind. To try to get at what this innovation means, I will describe the action of the first thirteen chapters of *The Scarlet Letter* from a standpoint which emphasizes their use of reciprocal responses on the part of the town and the principal characters.

A woman has borne a child and is judged adulterous. She is condemned by the rulers of a town islanded by the wilderness and the sea. The action of the rulers, who command both secular and spiritual authority, is an expression of corporate self-righteousness. Although we may question their judgment of Hester Prynne on both judicial and spiritual grounds, the book does not allow us to condone adultery. It is apparent from the outset that the sharp discrimination between Hester and the townspeople, which is signalized by the scarlet letter, has an unequivocal meaning only for the rulers of the town, and that Dimmesdale's view of her conduct is distinct from theirs. Of these rulers it is explicitly said that they are unfit to judge a woman's heart and, by an obvious extension, any grave sin. The judgment of Hester has the effect of unleashing the passions of many of the townspeople. Most seem to enjoy the moral holiday provided by a scapegoat. Instead of invoking divine assistance to keep them from similar transgressions, they tend to identify sinners with those whom their magistrates have punished. Some of the inhabitants have a superstitious awe of the letter and its wearer; Hester herself is made to perceive a sense of guilty participation in the faces of some of those she encounters, as if she were the embodiment of acts and impulses they do not confess. We move in these first thirteen chapters not so much through a fictional scene, although there are of course a number of set scenes, as through a field crisscrossed by the arrows of desire and impulse provoked by the presence of Hester wearing her letter. It is as if Hawthorne had fantasied the possibility of a diagrammatic completeness in noting these changes, exchanges, and transformations of emotional energy. We are licensed to push the notation further: for example, the response of Dimmesdale to his sense of transgression is to attack his own body; the response of the townspeople is to attack the separated member, the bearer of the stigma, the extruded evil. But I must carry my summary a little further.

The victim of moral exile is at the outset heavily burdened not simply by the sense of having injured her parents, her husband, and the innocent infant but by the loss of the whole nexus of sympathy and confidence which had united her to her fellows; putting it positively, there is an unbearable weight of antagonistic emotion under which she staggers. The cries of her infant reflect the passion with which she responds; Pearl is fed on embittered milk. The consequences of the experience of moral exile are for Hester herself wholly bad, despite the anomalous fact that they are publicly good. Hester Prynne's many charitable actions are devoid of any personal meaning; her apparent

rectitude becomes as hollow as the official self-righteousness of the elders—in fact, her response mirrors the terrible impersonality of the town's officialdom. It leads her to
think of the townspeople collectively, instead of as suffering and sinning individuals. The author's conclusion is
blunt: "The scarlet letter had not done its office." [12]
Hester's punishment leads her to imagine society in the
modern way, as a set of attitudes and powers which exert a
coercive power and from which she is wholly distinct, and
to bring to bear on this irrational, unjust, and inconsistent
entity her sense of outrage. She comes to feel that someday
the complementary invention, the individual, in particular
the individual woman, may serve as the prophetess who
frees her kind from the thralldom of society. Hester's
whole perspective on her world is analogous in its falsity
and abstractness to the perspective in which she has been
placed by those who judged her. Punished by the heads of
the community in accord with the terms of an ideology actually foreign to Christianity—they had not judged her,
but only the fact of her sin—Hester becomes as blind an
ideologue as they. But not openly, because she has a child,
and must, in behalf of the child's chance of rejoining the
community, behave as if its beliefs were hers. Even this
prudence is dictated by a mere hope for Pearl; despite the
presence of the wronged husband, and the man for whom
her love has been subdued and turned outward in hate of
her judges, her only tangible moral present lies in her relation to the child.

After a time Hester's behavior inspires a growing sentiment in her favor. The "great and warm heart" [13] which is
offered as a finally efficacious judge of conduct views her

as a chastened character. This public impression is errone-
ous. Moreover, Hester is not cherished for herself; rather,
her external sign, the letter, is changed in meaning. It becomes a symbol of her function, which we would call that
of a volunteer social worker. She refuses all offers of
friendship, and endures without any outward sign the
abuse of the lowly and the sly or cutting remarks of the
well born. Or, to put it in the offered paradigm, Hester's
outward charity is to her sin as Dimmesdale's hypocrisy is
to the fact of his guilt. Her response is a total and scornful
conformity to the ideal of selflessness; his is an exquisitely
tortured assertion of generic sinfulness which denies his
particular act. Both are generalized or abstract responses
to situations traditionally intelligible only as individual
cases of conscience. Such an account of a town, based
on reciprocal responses, of a community life which is the
result of interaction, is an extremity, almost (to paraphrase Emerson) a saturnalia or excess of faith in community as the nutrient bath of humanity.

Only of these first thirteen chapters may we say that the
dominant fictional mode is that of the paradigms, whether
of the order of tableau, as in the scene in which Hester
clutches her infant on the scaffold under the eyes of the
massed townspeople, or of the analytic sort, such as we get
in the thirteenth chapter itself, the notation of a charged
web of relationships, so tightly strung that, although
largely static, they are almost felt to thrum on the page.
The intensities seem not to lie in such moments of sce-
nically recorded anxiety and decision as Chillingworth's
interview with Hester in the prison, Hester's plea to retain
Pearl before Bellingham and Dimmesdale, or the minis-

ter's midnight vigil, but in the notation of the relationships which these scenes exhibit. This notation has carried us a long step beyond the fictional technique of the stories, in which we seldom quite escape the mode of *The Pilgrim's Progress*. Just as Christian encounters aspects of human behavior, so do Hawthorne and the reader of the stories meet a man who harbors a bosom serpent or wears a black veil or fantasies perfection for his lover. These joint encounters, in which writer and reader take the place of the audience to whom Bunyan appealed, likewise preclude any problem of moral judgment. The parable may be dusky to the reader, but he is tacitly burdened with the job of working it out in the terms Christian principle affords.

In the paradigmatic notation of this first structural block in *The Scarlet Letter*, moral problems arise at every turn, but we are given no assurance that resolution is at hand, if we could only invoke the imagination of charity. But a third view of human action is offered in the seventeenth, eighteenth, nineteenth, and twentieth chapters of *The Scarlet Letter*, a third fictional mode, which we may provisionally call dramatic. We do not make an immediate transition to a realized dramatic mode after the thirteenth chapter; the encounter between a paradigmatic Hester and a paradigmatic Chillingworth in Chapter Fourteen leads her to explain what sort of human abstraction she is and leads him to explain what sort of human abstraction he is. It is not a scene between a wife and a wronged husband meeting after seven years—in fact we have no ground for expecting it to be, since we have known Chillingworth simply as a realized consequence of the adultery; not as a separate fictional existence, but as a creature of whom cer-

tain qualities are initially specified and are thereafter recorded as interacting with those of Hester, Dimmesdale,
and the character of the town and its rulers. Yet when we
do reach the seventeenth chapter, it is as if the novel had
had a second illegitimate birth, as if it had been born into
the new world, once more masquerading, as it did the first
time, as a conformist's work, as if, to use our example, we
were still as safe as we are with Bunyan, instead of taking
all the risks of private judgment, as we must in Richard-
son's *Pamela*. We are in the presence of a man, a woman,
and a child, and we are free neither to judge them on the
basis of Christian assumptions nor to deny the necessity of
judging them. As readers we no longer have our hot little
hands in Hawthorne's; we are in an agonizing fix, a man is
loose, a woman is loose, and they are at the same time minister and parishioner, just as little Pearl is at the same time
fey creature of a disinherited fatherless antagonism to the
world and Dimmesdale's passionate child demanding a
father in the market place.

It is tempting to go further here with an analysis of the
action and try to write what so many people have tried un-
successfully to write, an account of what happens in *The
Scarlet Letter*. I shall return for just one note on the chapter called "The Minister in a Maze" at the end, but for the
moment I wish to make an additional remark about the
first thirteen. An account of their place in the action would
have to note that even in them the intervention of the
author takes a form distinct from the tough-minded oppositions set up by the paradigms. "The great and warm
heart," since it promises true judgment which will free us
from these inescapable oppositions, seems to beg the kind

of question raised by the thirteenth chapter: How can we envisage a resolution to the notations of an action which has made the town a worse town, Hester a worse woman, dehumanized Pearl, and driven Dimmesdale to make himself worse than a hypocrite by mingling his denial of his guilt with the town's denial of its part in Hester's sinfulness? In the "great and warm heart" we recognize an impulse to retreat from the harshness of this notation of the situation the paradigms create, and from the realized triumph of the book, the scenes in the wood which that notation makes possible. We must return to this retreat of Hawthorne's. But I wish first to deal with a more difficult question: How did Hawthorne come to construct his Boston?

We have to go all the way back to 1832, when *My Kinsman, Major Molineaux* was published, to find an earlier analogue to the fictional method of proportions or paradigms which is ascendant in the early chapters of *The Scarlet Letter*. And in that story the oppositions are presented emblematically, not as propositions. Was Hawthorne aware of the manner in which he had advanced beyond the technique of the stories? It is very hard to answer this question. The substitution of a Boston of his own creation—a town which he ruled absolutely, supplying not simply the overlay of morality and custom, but an account of the passional energies that these seek to control—for the world of the 1840's may have seemed a mere external requirement for the writing of a novel. (In this context *Fanshawe* surely didn't count for him.) I am inclined to believe that, had Hawthorne clearly realized the sequence of his movement from the method of the stories, which depended on Christian presumptions about his audience, to the paradigmatic notation of the first thirteen chapters of *The Scarlet Letter*, and then to the drama in the wood which these first thirteen chapters had somehow made possible, he would have betrayed more awareness of these shifts. In *The Scarlet Letter* Hawthorne appears to have come upon the possible consequences of his achieved freedom without full comprehension of the way in which he had achieved it. Hester and Dimmesdale and Pearl in the wood, outside the town in which their inner economy has been so fully noted, can draw upon something that none of Hawthorne's other characters have: a wholly comprehended inwardness. They need no Coverdale, who is essentially a bastard figure, both in and out of the novel, the figure of the man who is trying to make it all work though his very presence shows that it won't.

We may suppose, though I don't see how it can be proved, that in making the social and psychological notation he employed in *The Scarlet Letter*, Hawthorne had English novels in mind. In them the writer could employ his reader's awareness of the interplay between what had already been given public expression in relationships of class, an aspiring moneyed bourgeoisie, professional idioms, ethnic and cultural distinctions, a measure of historical awareness, and so on. By contrast, the paradigms, a logical extension of the Christian presumptions of the stories, had to be teased out of those presumptions and arrayed against the social climate of Massachusetts Bay as he envisioned it. Moreover, the resulting images of persons had to be brought into some relation with the presumptions about men, women, children and their relation to society in the 1850's. This necessity brings us back to the "great and warm heart." But I defer discussion of this once more in order to name some other conditions which were necessary to build Hawthorne's Boston.

D. H. Lawrence glimpsed one when, in writing about Hawthorne, he asserted the violent and destructive uses to which sexual energy may be put by a frustrated woman. He didn't quite know what Hawthorne was up to, but he saw this clearly. What Hawthorne had to find a form for was nothing less than a tale in which the root passion of man was related to the fact of community. It isn't simply the presence of explicit sexuality in the novel that is the basis of its power: it is the fact that Hawthorne brought civilization and sexuality face to face. It is perfectly clear (as John Thompson has pointed out) that long before Freud's *Civilization and Its Discontents* Hawthorne had reckoned with the heavy costs and the necessity of an accord between our passions and civil order.[14]

It may now make us wonder that a subject so broadly representative, so fatally American, didn't lead him into mere diffuseness. Was he not venturing on the territory which we see as occupied by those exploiters of the self, Emerson, Thoreau, and Whitman? That he wasn't entrapped into their spiritual imperialism we must attribute to a far surer sense of the primal conditions of selfhood than they possessed. In Hawthorne a man came to know himself through his relation to a woman, to parents, to children, to townsmen. Once you have met the other at your own hearth, you are immune to the diffuseness of transcendentalists and reformers. The system of referents which described a self might be hard to make, but it was not far to seek. The schematic accounts which stud the pages of *The Scarlet Letter* are so many efforts at describing selves through their enjoyed or suffered relationships. They make a structure of known selves and, as we have remarked, they make a bridge between the rather static moral pictures of the stories and the realized drama between the lovers which is at the heart of the novel.

Yet there is a rather striking discontinuity between stories, which have external moral sanctions, and the schematic relations of the novel, which are generated by the situation Hawthorne imagined. Hawthorne had taken the extraordinary step of locating the sanctions of morality within his action—and in doing so he opened the pathway which leads to *The Golden Bowl*. But he did not put the freedom he gained in this way to James's uses. *The Scarlet Letter* is much more closely akin to the novels of Jane Austen, George Eliot, or Trollope than it is to the late James. The Henry James who wrote a brilliant little essay in cultural contrasts and called it *Hawthorne* (1879) had earlier imitated the mode of Hawthorne's stories; he never saw the strength of *The Scarlet Letter*, or realized that his strictures on that work were to find a far juster application to a future work of his own, *The Golden Bowl*. He writes of the characters of *The Scarlet Letter:* "The people strike me not as characters, but as representatives, very picturesquely arranged, of a single state of mind; and the interest of the story lies, not in them, but in the situation, which is insistently kept before us, with little progression, though with a great deal, as I have said, of a certain stable variation; and to which they, out of their reality, contribute little that helps it to live and move." [15]

The writer of fiction in Hawthorne's century achieved that freedom which made him a novelist when the social forms of his age became the material of which he was master. There is no essential difference between Jane Austen's exquisitely modulated use of the marital maneuvers of country squires and Hawthorne's use of the Puritan ethos. These were the available traditions. His countrymen marched under the oriflamme of sin, guilt, and repentance. It was their most generally accepted version of themselves. The scarlet letter was not a widely resonant symbol, but a commonplace which Hawthorne made use of. But the fact that he did so does not mean that his difficulties in making a novel out of this matter were light. Jane Austen had the whole range of manners for her field; Hawthorne's countrymen offered him only the extremes of guilt and innocence. The paradigms had to supply the gradations between the extremes. What Hester came to feel about the townspeople and they about her was set down with great explicitness, an explicitness which had the effect of thickening the fictional medium. It is more than a figure to say that the paradigms are there to fill the vacant social space which lay between a morally exiled Hester and the publicly cherished appearance of Dimmesdale's sanctity. But a further proviso about the use of the paradigms belongs here: Hawthorne could not allow the reader to see that he was not fully in the writer's confidence, that the modified Bunyan mode had been abandoned, that the reader's moral assumptions were being used as material rather than as guides. To admit this would have meant an acknowledgment that in nature, men, and towns there were explosive energies at work which could not be articulated with the going social mores without pain and difficulty. This is that second illegitimate birth of the novel mentioned above. Hawthorne's "tale of human frailty and sorrow" [16] masquerades as a conformist's work. It involves an apparent paradox: our first great writer of fiction was our only great nineteenth-century figure whose allegiance to community was a primary imaginative commitment, and at the same time he was the first to make it plain that the energies that go into the making of each of us have anarchic possibilities. The waste, the frustration, the sorrow with which we bring the passions to heel emerged in *The Scarlet Letter* and covertly subverted all the current assumptions of fiction—that women were natively docile and sweet, that children were bucking to be angels, that a man in love was simply preparing to be a respectable householder.

I have been speaking as if Hawthorne's novel dealt with his contemporaries, as in fact it finally does. But it is laid in the New England past, which had made more than a formal profession of belief that men were fallen creatures. New England's history is one more of the necessary conditions of *The Scarlet Letter*. It was in itself a wonderful tale of spiritual adventure which had ended in something worse than the ideological tragedy Perry Miller describes; it had ended as Hawthorne saw it, in the spiritual and physical impoverishment he was at pains to point out in *The Scarlet Letter* and *The Blithedale Romance*. New England's women were no longer the vessels of passion; there was nothing burly or fanatically committed about those who lived there. Hawthorne borrowed that earlier society's explicitness and gusto to build the society of his book. The Puritans had loved venery and beef and ale and shining stuffs—their submission to the Lord had meant something. They had known temptation, and when they fell there had been a crash throughout the town of Boston. Hawthorne had no comprehension of their relish for savory doctrine; that in fact was what he found most frightening in them. What he sought and found was a world in which dramatic awareness of antinomies in human nature was the very ground on which a community was built.

The adventure of writing his tale became at the same time the adventure of imagining what his contemporaries could not give imaginative shape to: a town. In such an imagined town persons might exist because on that scene emotional realities would count, would make the crucial differences. Adultery would not lead to indifferent snickers; it would be an issue of life and death. The unbuttoned America Cooper's social novels exhibit could not be informed of its waste of human meaning and point by ideological tub-thumping. What in *The Blithedale Romance* was called "the mystic sensuality of this singular age" [17] was but one of a complex of attitudes which showed Hawthorne that his age was unable to locate personal and communal responsibility; unable to differentiate between human desire and natural force; unable, finally, to conceive of men as men and women as women.

If we now look back to our analysis of the first thirteen chapters, we can find the 1850's in what Hawthorne attributes to the mid-seventeenth century: Hester Prynne's distortion, her feminism, the emptiness of her categorization of Society as enemy of Woman, explains how injustice gives rise to distortion, and fosters it. If we also recall that the falsity and generality of Dimmesdale's behavior are one and the same—he denies Hester, Pearl, and the town, and does so to the effect of enhancing his own appearance of sanctity—we may see how immediately Hawthorne was able to dramatize the evil of abstract thought or of blanket conclusions. In this context the customary mad scientist, Chillingworth, is hardly so threatening an evil as is the impersonality which is seen to characterize all the wickedness of *The Scarlet Letter* as it crops up in Hester, the town, Pearl, and Dimmesdale—even Pearl becomes frightening because she is faced not by persons but by massed antagonism on the part of the children. We can also recognize an explanation for something that has perhaps puzzled us about *The Scarlet Letter:* Hawthorne's impulse to accord the "great and warm heart" a final efficacy, and to blur the last days of Hester Pyrnne by suggesting that what has distorted her has in some actual measure made her a prophetess, as if the rights of women were indeed a Hawthorne cause. He has responded to his age by invoking a false generality, cobbling up a religion of his own. He fought his age with the paradigms, but fudged the struggle at crucial moments. He was not always brave. In fact, he was never really brave in this fashion again. In *Blithedale* he carries on with the indictment of an age in which persons are no longer related through their truly human energies, but he does so at one remove: his form and his utopian colony fail to come together to release those energies which were so triumphantly at play for a few chapters in *The Scarlet Letter*.

The scene in the wood between Hester and Dimmesdale and, later, Pearl, is the closest approach to the actualities of passion between grown men and women our nineteenth-century novels managed. We can hardly exaggerate the courageousness of Melville's desperate effort to confront such matters in *Pierre*, but brave as it is, it does not succeed. Hawthorne for one moment, and after an extraordinarily elaborate set of preliminary maneuvers, managed what no one else could, a scene in which human greatness, pathos, and failure are based upon what is inescapable about the characters: that he is a man, she a woman, Pearl their child, and all three must encounter a human world into which the consequences of passion, copulation, birth, and growing up must somehow be fitted. So resonant is this encounter that conventional analyses of the book's design amount to denials of its felt force for the reader. The imaginative generosity involved in the creation of three persons who are allowed to stand free, to live and move and have their being in a dramatic context, was very great indeed. This must have been the bitter measure of the failure of *The Blithedale Romance* for Hawthorne; Zenobia also has her scene in the wood, but neither he nor his reader can feel assured that there is anyone for her to encounter, and without such an encounter the book falls back on notation, assertion, paradigm.

I wish to return once more to *The Scarlet Letter*'s twentieth chapter, "The Minister in a Maze." It is axial to Frederick Crews's reading of the book, and to mine. In brief, the question is whether Dimmesdale, once he has agreed to flee overseas with Hester and has returned to Boston, writes his sermon as a man who, having deliberately erred, is now for the first time a man who can choose the right path—or is, as Crews sees him, libidinally inspired, capable of what we may call instant sublimation.[18] Hawthorne says of Dimmesdale's consent to accompany Hester, "he had yielded himself with deliberate choice, as he had never done before, to what he knew was deadly sin . . ."[19] As he makes his way home he is, as Crews says, "blessed with a new energy of body and will." He is bubbling with impulses to corrupt maidens and blast the faith of trustful old women. He thereupon sits down to a fresh Election Sermon, having discarded the first draft, and writes what three days later will, on the book's unimpeachable authority, be the most deeply affecting performance of his career, and the one which we must think of as having realized the author's famous injunction to "be true," even though it precedes the actual confession on the scaffold. Crews says, "There is no doubt that Dimmesdale has recovered his piety in the three days that intervene between the writing of the sermon and its delivery." But of the sermon itself, Crews writes, "In short, the Election Sermon is written by the man who wants to corrupt young girls in the street, and the same newly liberated sexuality 'inspires' him in both cases."[20] How the man who has recovered his piety can bear to utter a tainted sermon Crews doesn't explain.

As in the case of *Young Goodman Brown*, it is necessary to remind Crews that when we are dealing with drama, changes are dramatic, and that when we are dealing with Hawthorne's Christian notation of moral event, we must concede a difference between sin and guilt. To recognize himself as a deliberate sinner is for Hawthorne's character to become at last, and for good, a citizen, a member of a community of men who err, and who, unlike the polar character he has been and Hester remains, walks the middle zone of error and repentance. It is a man, not a fake saint or a lecher, who writes the sermon.

The peculiarly asocial, ahistorical character of Crews's study of Hawthorne raises a question of general interest about the literary analyst who employs Freudian notions without being able to believe that there is—or was!—any analogue of Vienna out there into which either patient or book may be discharged. In such an age all psychoanalytic procedures are interminable because the world into which the patient was formerly discharged has so largely melted away—not that society doesn't exist in a fashion, but the energies of belief in it as a scene of the consummations of work and love have sunk very low.

Hawthorne was very much aware of an earlier stage in the process by which we have fallen out of love with society on this continent. (My "we" is of course a reference to commanding imaginations, and not a dated sociological judgment.) Both in *The Scarlet Letter* and in *The Blithedale Romance* his primary focus was on the character and strength of the bonds that unite men, women, and children in a society and how they may and must be used to constrain the imperious inward demands of fantasy and obsession, which, as Crews makes plain, Hawthorne habitually saw as rooted in sexual struggles. That Hawthorne went much further than Crews sees in consciously reckoning with the problems created by imperious inward demands and the needs of a social order is not surprising, because Crews seems wholly to lack any assurance that there is or was a scene on which these claims might have been adjudicated within or without fiction.

If we contrast Hawthorne with Emerson for a moment,

we may glimpse what is at issue more clearly. Emerson's proclamation that the man who entered into the inward empire and forgot external claims was not only guiltless, but would discover that he had inherited all that had formerly been expressed in the divided and fragmented social and sexual roles is precisely what Hawthorne denied, not only in *The Celestial Railroad*, but in the very structure of *The Scarlet Letter*. If we had read only the stories Hawthorne wrote before *The Letter*, we might feel licensed to conclude that any claim to be a self and enact inner demands made one guilty, aberrant, destructive, because it cut us off from our fellows. But we have more than the stories to deal with; *Blithedale* and *The Scarlet Letter* made it plain that to aspire to the generic roles, that of a man, a woman, of that nascent grownup, a child, is not intially to be guilty. It is in these novels that we see that Hawthorne did more than invert the Emersonian assertion. The guilt incurred by the splendid male, Hollingsworth, or the pinched, impotent, and keen-witted Chillingworth may seem to be in the vein of the stories. But it is distinct for two allied reasons: in each case the claims of a woman to enact her role have been defeated by a man, and in each case the social conditions deny men the chance to be fully men and women the chance to be fully women. Hawthorne made community central and indispensable; he did not see any way to transcend it, but he was not inclined to give it a blanket endorsement, even in its more explicitly human seventeenth-century guise. We must concede that in the persons of the splendid, and to most critics inexplicable, women, Hester and Zenobia, we find proof of the measure in which Hawthorne's imagination was not simply sexualized but socialized. No matter how dark they may be, they make the claim of a woman in whom we may say the Oedipally split roles of the unclean and fatally attractive dark lady and the virginally fair lady have been recombined; they make a claim for a husband and a community which glory in both their sexuality and their fostering power. Their defeat is not offered in Hawthorne's fiction as the defeat of a fantast, or of one obsessed: the claim they make on us is rendered as generic, the claim of kind.

The Hawthorne described in this chapter is almost unrecognizable in what has been written about him in the last two generations. But of course the last two generations lacked our awareness of the realization of the imaginative process of disaffiliation from society. They also held it illicit to argue from the writer's work to the loves and commitments of the writer. The belief that this prohibition arose simply out of our discovery of a theory of literature is of course simply fallacious. Such theories have been used to justify our abstemiousness, but the fact is that it arose out of our passional death to two tremendous nineteenth-century inventions: the concept of society and the concept of history. To employ these in connection with literary study would have been to profess loves we no longer felt. Yet if society was earlier viewed, as Hawthorne viewed it, as the unique ground of our triumphs and defeats, we can only falsify the perspectives of fiction which accepted this view by subjecting them to our loss of faith. Challenged as to where they had put humanity, those two critical generations might have replied: on the top shelf, out of reach of time and circumstance, in those literary works which have been granted a certificate of total imaginative coherence. That coherence Hawthorne did not have. It wasn't form that he loved most. He tried with a noble generosity to imagine a world in which other persons really counted.

Chapter III

Consciousness and Form in Whitman

Our ability to disguise the fact that Emerson and Whitman were deeply subversive, not simply of existing social arrangements but of society itself, would seem astonishing if those who discussed them had put it before us squarely. But they have not because they have been carrying on the enterprise of the imperial self themselves. By the time we were ready to confront the texts we were so caught up in the religion of art, the assertion of the sufficiency and finality of form, that we had simply turned these two prophets into more or less successful artists. In the case of Emerson, this has led to substantial distortion and failure to recognize his cultural meaning; in that of Whitman, the question is more complicated in the degree that his works may be considered apart from his effort to create a new kind of consciousness.

To say that a movement in literary criticism has made an important social assertion without awareness of the fact, that the religion of art is the unacknowledged successor to the prophetic office of Emerson and Whitman, is not to deny the efficacy and power of that movement when it is performing its ostensible task. But when its techniques are applied to writers who do not satisfy its criteria of formal adequacy, and these writers are then viewed as definable simply in the terms criticism now offers, the effect is a cultural and historical smear, a confusion. No such misapplication of technique has taken place in our commentary on larger figures such as Augustine, Swift, Rousseau, or Nietzsche. They are seen to be both commanding imaginations and figures inseparable from their cultural situation; they are not stretched on the rack of formal adequacy.

Our impulse to extend certain critical techniques indiscriminately has roots we don't understand, and these are to be found in our conception of humanity. I close the circle, or attempt to, by suggesting that these needs are in fact the same needs that Emerson and Whitman themselves manifest: the needs of the imperial self. (A discussion of the relationship between the religion of art and our prophets is undertaken in the last chapter.)

To return to Whitman: if we really face what we have done with this poet, we must admit that we have done something ordinarily regarded as no longer possible—we have committed a humanistic sin. Criticism of Whitman which catches him up in the context of the religion of art has the intention of defining terminal experiences afforded by his poetry and outlining its formal sufficiency as the

vehicle of such experiences. But to assert the adequacy of a
form which is in fact not present, while treating works that
are major accomplishments in the definition of a new form
of consciousness, is worse than error: it is the newest of
the treasons of the clerks. A poem is, so to speak, a partial
act, and prophecy is a total act. We have mistaken the
character of Whitman's activity.

America has no patent on any form of consciousness; we
do have a historically important chronological priority in
the case of the kind of consciousness this book is about.
We did not succeed in giving that consciousness form in
poetry during our nineteenth century. That happened first
in Europe, and Rilke was a central figure in this context.
Rilke did have a formal sufficiency which licenses us to
give ourselves up to him completely while we read;
through its very imaginative independence, his work can
deliver us to a world of other existences, if we seek such
deliverance. But to say that Whitman's work is in this
sense free of its maker is like saying that we have had *an*
experience of the incarnation. For this reason it is useful to
keep Emerson in view while discussing Whitman; both
were first figures in the culture and then makers.

Questions of perspective are crucial here. From our post-
modernist standpoint, Emerson's negation of society was
something far more important than an effort on the part of
a dying agrarian community to preserve its psychic elbow
room. To put that negation and Hawthorne's rather muted
affirmation at the center of the stage is required by the
awareness that the post-modernist period enforces. Our interest in the past is now explicitly shaped by the fact that a
large process is seen to be concluding: society as Emerson

knew it has almost ceased to exist, and the ties that now bind us do not make the same claims nor have the same functions in establishing individual identities. The death of the social ideal in certain nineteenth-century imaginations seems much more momentous than it did when these writers were regarded as splendid sports rather than the forerunners of a coming actuality. When that actuality found specific forms in European works of art, the most striking and complete evidence of our desocialized state emerged, after the work of Emerson, Thoreau, and Whitman was done. The European works have an authority far greater than that of our writers simply because of their greater measure of formal realization; they can be considered apart from the persons who created them as almost no work of Emerson's or Whitman's can. The authority these latter have for us is largely the personal authority of figures in the culture. Without that dimension they cease to be Emerson and Whitman and become the puppets of literary-critical fashion. The influence of that fashion is still so strong that I should warn the reader that I am not telling him that Emerson and Whitman are unimportant, but that they are important in a neglected dimension. The warning is necessary because it is still true for every literate person except a youth in revolt that the authority of persons over his imagination is not as great as that of works of art. It is a well-kept secret essential to understanding the cultural moment that those over thirty who are occupied with literature believe works of art to be more real than life.

We think of Whitman as a poet whose works can be separated one from another. At his best he is the author of this poem or that, and cannot be discussed, as Emerson can, with an eye chiefly to the producing cause, Emerson, and his aims vis-à-vis an audience. Brilliant as Emerson was, he was not the *poet* of his own program; Whitman, within the limits I wish to suggest, was that poet, although his best poems are read uncomprehendingly by those who do not see him as the prophet of a particular kind of consciousness.

Whitman was surely a big leap forward in our imaginative desocialization; perhaps the most notable of all. How did he become possible? The question isn't fully answerable, but some of the elements of an answer may be suggested. Emerson seems to have been a necessary condition, and a crude formula might run: Emerson plus an active sensuality leads to the possibility of a Whitman. But Emerson had developed a socially accepted role by easy stages and found the lyceum prepared for him. He became preacher to the nation. Whitman had no such assurance that any of his occupations would offer a bridge to a new kind of part on the American scene. To have been a carpenter, school teacher, journeyman printer, newspaper editor, dandy, and hack writer did not in any instance offer an open road to what he felt himself capable of and finally achieved. It was rather by negating the implications of these occupations than, as in Emerson's case, by developing the potentialities of one occupation that Whitman became Whitman. It was a greater feat than our idioms have made it easy for us to say. The recent discovery of his emotional ups and downs, his despair, his gaiety, his wit, and his verbal energy, for which we have to thank Schyberg, Asselineau, Chase, Jarrell, and R. W. B. Lewis, has not revealed and has even temporarily prolonged our failure to apprehend his cultural significance. It was his discovery of the possibility of living and writing in accord with the Emersonian program that made him what he became. Living it, we may say, in his poems, adopting it as a psychic stance, or finding it a model expression of his native psychic stance.

His newness was so simple and so massive a thing that statements about it are hard to frame. To take up Emerson's challenge was to write as if the world were literally your oyster. No forecast of the behavior of the future citizens of the republic, not even Tocqueville's, had prepared anyone for the man who made it his premise that there was nothing to do but celebrate himself. His inability to perform any specified task to his or anyone else's satisfaction is patent. But the brilliant inversion that made apparent weakness strength is our puzzle. Such a capacity for conscious self-acceptance is surely rare. One can express the contraries logically: If I'm nobody in your eyes, I am at least everybody in my own. But logic doesn't go far. The parallel with Henry James's account of himself is useful. Whitman's was surely a "visiting mind" [1] which ended by absorbing and interpreting all those existences heretofore so strikingly authoritative over him, including, in Whitman's case, the shabbiest of current literary modes. Both men transformed and ordered to their own use what had initially seemed overwhelming. In both it was a case of all or nothing: a total imaginative victory or a total artistic and personal defeat. To make use of the world was to render it tributary to the empire of the self without giving any hostages. To make the firmament your drum; to make it resound to your message as if there were no interposing persons or resistances of any sort. This was almost a formula for the imaginative strain we are following.

Or we can turn the question about and consider the way in which the whole middle ground of traditional roles, where the ordinary business of the society and the species is carried on, is occupied. Or, rather, not occupied, but turned into your material so that it is not thought of as compelling but becomes your possession. If you are Whitman, how do you begin to do this? We should scarcely know had Whitman not done it: you write "Song of Myself," you put all other existences into solution. The great exemplary Whitman poem is "Crossing Brooklyn Ferry," because it is most explicit about the meaning of being dissolved as Whitman sought to dissolve us. To be "struck from the float," [2] to be an image in the water from which radiates the whole of being, is to be no more significantly bound to one person than another, to have nothing left but your body and your imputed universality. Whitman offered the sensation of lapsing into everything as the greatest of gifts; he was the prime poet of uncreation. Like a shaman making a puppet to represent the enemy to be destroyed, he dowers his world with only so much quiddity as he can dissolve, or cants each created thing on the slope of process down which it will slide to oblivion. In "Crossing Brooklyn Ferry," he deprived himself and all the rest of us of generational place and put everything into the eternal moment of the sunset, ferries, gulls, and radiating images in the water.

But I ought to say more about the manner before discussing the effect of Whitman's poetry. He was, first of all, a literalist about his own emotional universe. Before he ever undertook the poems for the 1855 edition, we may be quite sure, he had apprehended the world in the terms they disclose. A poem, in other words, was not a separate emotional storm which found its form, like a dream stranded in the daylight of print. The dream went on all day, and the poem was that raid on actuality or nameable circumstance which clothed it for print. The quality of Whitman's revisions shows this. They were not dictated by a sense of the integrity of the object, but by the current mode of his exhibition of the pervasive and enduring dream. Poets of the orchestra, the dancing-place of communal life, such as Wordsworth or Yeats, write from the middle ground on which others appear. They have made the enormous concession, unrealized in Whitman's imagination, that one exists in one's relation to other persons. They were not born of "perfect" mothers, but of particular mothers. It is, I believe, a central observation about Whitman that he undermined such structures as are said to be the basis of signification in Lévi-Strauss' *Savage Mind*.[3] His use of species was not to discriminate, his use of human functions and relations had the end of agglomeration, his use of place did not effect distinctions. To put it generally, his universe is one in which particular acts which terminate in a changed relationship among things signified are made formally unthinkable. It is mere grammatical pedantry to think of his catalogues as having the end of inclusion: at their brilliant best, they are successful efforts to melt things together, to make the sum of things ring with one note.

These raids on actuality resulted in poems which touch us deeply, although in a sharply limited way. Their pathos, their delicate nostalgia, and their comedy are intimate reminders of the inclusive assertions we made before the world became hopelessly plural—or gloriously dramatic. Earlier readers tended to accept or reject Whitman on grounds that now seem quite external. Cultural subversion as profound and inclusive as Whitman's cannot be countered directly until the issues it raises are perceived. Whitman is no longer subversive; his prophecy has been in a considerable degree fulfilled. Although *Leaves of Grass* is in fact an assault on a world of dramatically realized roles, the family constellation, rooted distinctions of every sort, even D. H. Lawrence's recognition of the fact, strident though it was, was successfully blurred by F. O. Matthiessen and others. (The positive welcome extended by Swinburne seems wholly in accord with his own appetite for object-erosion and emotional diffuseness.) But Whitman did not actually find a welcoming climate until the 1940's and 1950's. He was then finally apprehended in a cultural context in which his assault on the grown-up self was welcome. The disappearance of articulate awareness of a place in a social scheme and the concomitant substitution on the part of his readers of objects of art for history made this easy. Those who wrote about Whitman were unaware of the cultural changes which had made it possible for the first time to accept him unreservedly.

But we must keep reminding ourselves that the conditions under which the imperial self asserted its powers in Emerson, Whitman, and Thoreau were those of conflict with a culture they viewed as adversary. When the conflict lapsed a hundred years later, the latter two got academic recognition in the measure that they were graced by literary form.

But these academic acknowledgments of Whitman are, in the history of our culture, a secondary manifestation. Those whose welcome was direct, Henry Miller, Norman O. Brown, the beats of the 1950's, are openly and gratefully aware of Whitman as a cultural ancestor. Together with the elder Henry James, they may be used to suggest how apocalyptic Whitman was for his own day, and how much of his power has been disguised or transformed by his academic sponsors. Brown and Miller and Allen Ginsberg quite simply know what sort of human assertion Whitman was making and celebrate that assertion. For these admirers of Whitman the totalitarianism of the self is the enjoyed and acted-on mode of human vision.

Brown's sense of kinship with Whitman is accurate. In fact, *Love's Body* makes it appear that despite his impulse toward an orgiastic apocalypse, made quite explicit after the appearance of *Life Against Death*, the proper epigraph for his work is the fifth section of "Song of Myself," in which the shudder in the loins engenders a verbal structure, a world in which actual revolutionary change is unthinkable. The program of apocalyptic social transformation in *Life Against Death* is retreated from in *Love's Body*, a book in which Brown appears to have confided all the possibilities of social change to the power of art to transform consciousness. This second book celebrates passivity, as does Whitman's fifth section. This part of Whitman's poem is a waking wet dream in which one is ravished by the universe. Delighted passivity and megalomaniacal assertion: it was almost a formula for American genius of the strain we are following.

I mean to use Brown for documentary purposes, but I ought first to acknowledge that he is much more than a symptom. It isn't improper to speak of him as the American Nietzsche, although the adjective must also serve to indicate that he is a lesser figure. He is not simply brilliant on Swift and Luther, he is the kind of visionary who reveals cultural actualities. His use of Freud is an attempt to repel the Viennese invader with American weapons: it is as if America had at last responded with its own voice to Freud's account of the world in which the family constellation and individual psychic histories are primary; in Brown the undifferentiated self fights back. We approach here the most important commonplace of studies of American national character. Reuel Denney summarized it in 1960: "A student of American character may say, as he usually does, that the American is more American in his adolescence than at any other time in his life." He goes on, "Another way of putting this is to say that in later life the American is most American when he shows traces of an adolescence not left behind." [4] These "traces" take form in our writers. They make of the roleless role, of the undifferentiated self, more than it can be in any actual human existence. They project the shadow of the imperial self out of their circumstanced lives. Brown's celebration of the body of delight, the stage of the polymorphously perverse infant, in *Life Against Death*,[5] is the fantasy of an adolescent sensibility carried to the point of rebellion against our physiological differentiation into sexes. It is an exemplary grown-up's revolt, which finds its expression through the

avenue of surviving adolescent feelings. It should be said
that this point of intersection with studies of national character is momentary and, strictly, accidental, for it is the
quality of the humanity of the writers with whom we are
dealing that engages me here, together with the widespread assumption that they are indeed representative.
One might of course broaden the application by treating
more writers whom we have judged peculiarly our own.[6]

The vision to which Freud provokes Brown is an account of western character structure in which Freud's scientific concerns and the therapeutic goals of satisfying
work and object-love become signs of distortion and subjection to a fundamentally anal culture. (Brown's own distortion of Freud is considerable but intelligible, because
consonant with the emotional project I am describing.)
Boehme and Blake are of great importance to Brown. His
direct American predecessor, doctrinally, is the elder
Henry James.[7] Brown proposes and announces a collective psychoanalysis of western man, a generic return of the
repressed which will put an end, as will a similarly collective process in the elder Henry James, to paternalistic religion, the state, and history. Fourier lies behind the "spiritual socialism" of the elder James, as Marx does behind
Brown's project for a collective salvation. For Brown both
our personalities and our culture are representations of ascendant anal impulse. Although the elder Henry James,
following Swedenborg, saw his apocalypse as the end of
an anally qualified civilization all of whose evils were to be
defecated through the church, the cloaca of self-righteousness, or, in the case of the individual, the expulsion of the
selfhood (familiar in Blake's use of it), he did not con-

demn a genitally localized sexuality, as does Brown. But the elder James accomplished a similar psychic redisposition by calling for the abolition of "famished appetite and mercenary lust" [8] and envisaging a new form of relationship between male and female which finds the accustomed physiological expression but is bathed in a different awareness on the part of the man, that in making love to the woman he is in fact paying tribute to our "spiritual manhood" [9] of which she is the manifestation. This denial of the finally bipolar character of sexuality was accompanied by scorn for the Catholic attack on the "procreative faculty" [10] manifest in the rule of celibacy for the priesthood, and for prudishness in general. Brown and the elder James are again at one in their attack on the belief that scientific positivism and the Kantian intuitions represent finalities. As James put it: "Space and time are really mental substances having no other function than to compel all the objects of Nature and all the events of history into the compass of the human form." [11] (There is an embarrassment of associations with Blake here. It should be explained, although we can't now follow the argument, that the modifications of Swedenborg to be found in both Blake and the elder Henry James are similar in important respects, especially in that they both shift the focus from the angels to man, and more especially still to man as creative.) Although in the elder James it was only through man's exercise of his power that the "divine-natural humanity" might be realized—that the god now wholly shut up within us might be freed—he did not go so far as to make the human imagination the sole creative agency, as did Blake. Both James and Brown conceive death as the death to our true fulfillment to which our present deformations condemn us, and in both science and acquisitiveness are the engines of this deformation.

In one familiar way Brown simply recapitulates Boehme, Blake, and Swedenborg in making the history of mankind parallel the history of the individual. By adding this parallelism to his version of Freud, Brown makes Freudian thought essentially religious and takes it altogether out of the realm of the therapeutic or scientific. Our humanity cannot be recaptured piecemeal by individuals. Self-confrontation with our presently deformed selves within the social medium is the only road, in both Brown and the elder James, to a collective salvation.

There is every ground for thinking of Brown—or one of his admirations, Henry Miller—as carrying out Whitman's implied cultural program. Despite his emphasis on the body of delight, Brown is akin to Emerson as well as Whitman. The likeness is a consequence of an impulse to undo society imaginatively. Behind the screen lurk the gigantesque claims of the infantile self, in Emerson, in Whitman, in Brown, in Henry Miller. Whitman spoke as these writers do for his pervasive dream, but its episodes are more often set apart by the shape he gave them; he was, in a greater measure than Emerson, committed to form, committed to something other than the tradition Frank Kermode describes in *Romantic Image*, but nonetheless known by something separable from his history and his impulses. Recognition by cultural descendants, recognition by critics—we have to deal with both if we are to encounter Whitman now. The critics have been busy cobbling Whitman into apprehensible shape, reading him for linguistic triumphs and finding enough to reassure themselves that he may be read in the mode in which we read art that is safely lodged in its form. But it hasn't quite worked, cannot in fact finally work. The proof is that it so often focuses on the wrong poems. Whitman remains both in and out of the game. We can proceed only if we examine the imaginative departure from Emerson, and not simply the approximations to commitment to form. We have to approach from the direction of Whitman's disposition of his emotional energies. (This is evidenced though not acknowledged in the sequence of discussion in recent years —first the biographical work of Schyberg and Asselineau then the first full-dress attempts at criticism.[12]) We must see what he added to Emerson and how it transformed the Emersonian enterprise. It was of course his own body which was his prime instrument of discovery. In Blake this is conscious and fully articulated; in Whitman, although the primacy of the body is often proclaimed, the consequences must in part be inferred from the poetic texture.

Before leaving the Blake comparison, I note that it is, at least as a start, useful to think of Whitman as Harold Bloom thinks of Blake, as asserting a world of subjects as against a world of objects, or a world imaginatively dominated by objects and rational thought about objects.[13] (To push this hard would be misleading, if only because Whitman had no clear sense of the meaning of a Blakean attempt to write and feel in a nonempirical mode.) The body Whitman sought to realize was his own; he was not a romantic in what may after all be the primary sense: that he offered a world *over against* the objects, convictions, states of feeling, and personalities of the world in which he moved. The difficulty of the material was denied by Emerson and Whitman; they would overcome disparity by incorporation, not by any form of temporally qualified dialectic of the imagination. Whitman sought to occupy the indefinitely extensible imperium of his own body. He perceived others not as sharing a shape, not as objects out there, but as sharing powers to sing, to walk, to lounge, to fuse or to agglomerate. The existence of other persons is only marginally and thinly established in Whitman's works, and the terms in which all but a very few appear are genteelly or sentimentally conventional. In isolation they would resemble the sentimental observations of contemporary magazine fiction. I speak of the look of others, the loves and actions of others. The boy and the red-faced girl sneaking into the bushes, John Paul Jones, the competitors at the turkey shoot, the dying man borne to the hospital in a litter; these stories or vignettes suffer from their distancing, their higher degree of objectification, as against the blacksmiths at the forge, the driver of the omnibus with his "interrogating thumb," [14] or the Negro drayman, all instances in which, as in the manifold movements which enter into "Crossing Brooklyn Ferry," we enter the flux of being of which Whitman's body is the sentient crossroad.

The dislimning of persons which is notable in Whitman is not present in Emerson; he could hit off a character in a brilliant way because acknowledgment of the physical presence and characteristic gestures of others did not so directly threaten his mode of generalizing his world, possessing his world; "soul" was the theater of secular incarnation. But in Whitman it was the body. Within the theater of soul Emerson's greater and lesser, atemporal and temporal "egos" carried on their play; Whitman's sense of his body and the imaginative uses of his body were not of a commensurate order in all ways; his use of the term "soul" was rather strictly correlative with the sum of appearances he had at any moment invoked. He was hospitable to a variety of impulses in himself which he attributed to others. He leafed out souls in mimicry of the world of social roles. Some he made, some he borrowed, as when he assumed the persona of the young woman watching the twenty-eight bathers. These tropisms were matched by a pseudopodial withdrawal as well; incorporation and even engorgement qualified the body which was the poet's scene. We can find many poems which this description does not fit because they depend on more external modes that distance the world through childhood reminiscence or the use of borrowed fictions. But the process I have sketched is the one which characterizes his best work.

Whether we follow Wilhelm Reich, Norman O. Brown, or simply our most general awareness of the traffic between psyche and soma, we are of course aware that the body is shaped by cultural use and expectation. The labor I have attributed to Whitman is therefore a labor of undoing, unmaking, not simply a stepping out of doors all naked. We may speak of Whitman's narcissism if we like, but it must be premised that its consequence is not that which we observe in the professional models on television, whose narcissism is exploited by a cultural form, and who seem somehow deader than corpses. Whitman's narcissism was a communicated delight in the fat sticking to his bones; it was very far from a lapse into a solipsism. The culture had found no voice for it earlier; a delighted self-absorption was in theory reserved to God, but hadn't been emotionally realized in the world of art or practice. Indeed, the very act of proclaiming it to oneself was carried out in the presence of the superego, was in its conception quasi-public already. It was a species of horizontal subversion theoretically available to everybody yet in practice open to very few because the psychic resistance to it was massive. The notion of rejoicing in the odor of one's own armpits, had it been widely apprehended, would undoubtedly have provoked mass retching.

What to do with such disturbing emotions? Well, the obvious recourse, if you responded to Whitman's power, was to tuck him into a category in which he might appear less alarming than he was. Whitman aiding, you could treat him as a "rough," an individualist, a living proof of America's power to foster independence. The moral and political commitment to the value of individuals his countrymen had formally subscribed to could be employed to cancel the terrifyingly immediate level on which some of Whitman's poetry spoke to its readers. This first disposition of Whitman still confuses our apprehension of the emotional universe his poetry institutes. The contemporary habit of emphasizing those Whitman works which, like "Out of the Cradle," distance and control the full force of his dream, together with emphasis on Whitman's valuable democratic singularity, still obscures his definition as a cultural force. One way to explore the character of this

force is to ask what existences he was prepared to acknowledge in the world about him. If he was the poet of
his dream and not a maker of images, who was permitted
to figure in it? Popular figures and stereotypes of character in city and country were liberally employed in *Leaves
of Grass*, but if one considers these other centers of senti-
ence with a view to the poetic intensity with which they
were invoked, they quickly dwindle in number and specificity. The scale of emotional intensity falls away toward
zero when it is a question of fathers. ("On the Beach at
Night" is the poet's address to the child within.) Mothers,
reduced to a generic fostering function, children, "com-
rades," human beings subdued into oneness by sleep or
death, the lover, chronologically confined to 1856–60,
whose kiss validates reality, these are figures heavily
charged for Whitman (Lincoln is less of an exception than
he appears). The Whitman to whom these human functions and relations appeared was a man peculiarly unshel-
tered by his own explicit role, one who was either lover of
the world or nothing. The completeness of object-erosion
in him is striking. Nothing could be farther removed from
our sense of him than the ability to call up the quiddity of
things or individuals, times, or places. Objects are put before us for the purposes of assimilation.

Reference to Wordsworth is again helpful. Like other
romantic poets, he was sometimes struck all of a heap by
the fact of other identities, by their profound remoteness
and unknowability. The beggar whom, in "The Prelude,"
he encounters in London is wearing a placard which announces him, but how can the poet bridge the awful gap

created by the sheer otherness of another existence? Can we ever know more than the placard proclaims? It seems possible to account for this romantic experience culturally. Theirs was an age, the first age, in which other persons could have appeared unsupported by, unconstrained by, a known social part. Wordsworth's peculiar liability to invasion by a sense of the possibly countervailing grandeur of others is familiar. The old Cumberland beggar, the soldier encountered at night in *The Prelude*, the leech gatherer, all offered themselves with an authority which so far transcended ostensible role as to defy immediate explanation. The terrifying openness of a world in which people have begun to be invaded by a sense of the mysteries of identity is all there. But in Whitman the response was lacking or, significantly, was represented as overwhelming, as it is in "The Sleepers." To Wordsworth these experiences were challenges, challenges to which we can see him rising in the magnificent "Idiot Boy" or in "Simon Lee." In these works the other was entertained, was related to the poet's sensibility and dealt with by his powers. The dark side of Whitman found in "The Sleepers" was precisely the terror of the overmastering authority of other existences. He was alone, in the open, exposed by homosexual emotion to a world in which he had no defined or accepted place. To survive he had to subdue all other existences to himself. No serial encounters were possible to him. The dream was in this sense finally defensive—was, in other words, a dream. Like Emerson he had to be an optimist.

But out of the possible defeat the triumph came about.

Whitman loved himself enough, loved himself splendidly, and he succeeded often enough to become a great celebrant of his imperium of body and soul:

> *In me the caresser of life wherever moving,*
> *backward as well as forward sluing,*
> *To niches aside and junior bending, not a*
> *person or object missing,*
> *Absorbing all to myself and for this song.*
>
> ("*Song of Myself*," *from Section 13*)

> *The light and shade, the curious sense of body*
> *and identity, the greed that with perfect*
> *complaisance devours all things,*
> *The endless pride and outstretching of man,*
> *unspeakable joys and sorrows,*
> *The wonder everyone sees in everyone else he*
> *sees, and the wonders that fill each minute*
> *of time forever . . .*
>
> ("*A Song for Occupations*," *from Section 3*)

We shall come round to it in time: "Out of the Cradle" is very touching, very appealing, has something of the ordering within the work that makes poems hang together as independent objects, but it is not really a patch on "Song of Myself," in which Whitman's distortion becomes exemplary, becomes American, is in fact the rather awesome realization of the cost and the glory of being enough for oneself, of living in the momentaneous, of living in the body conceived and felt as the sufficient paradigm of existence. Now that we have found the line "I find I incorporate gneiss," [15] to be comic, we are perhaps ready to admit that it is serious. (Earlier it was presumably felt to be just blather.) Or are we not ready to admit that it is serious because it isn't an "artifice of eternity," [16] an image we can really single out? It is a part of my purpose in this essay to find a vocabulary in which we can call it serious. To do so is to embrace the problem of writing about a man who is at once a poet and a cultural figure, both in and out of the game of criticism as we have been playing it.

It is not of course quite to finish with the question of the poetic mode to call the line I have quoted "serious." It is, we may say, a mode we must distinguish from the comic or elegiac because such modes have an ineradicable tie to ways of encountering life which have been elaborated by culture. Whitman, literalist of his emotional universe, did sometimes fall back on such modes, but he was not doing so here; he was playing one of those brilliant tunes on himself which characterize his best work; genial and terrified, he is living the life which E. M. Forster attributed as a momentary experience to the old man in "The Road from Colonus," who, standing within the great hollowed-out tree from which the spring flows, found himself in the tide of being moving toward death. [17]

We come back finally to D. H. Lawrence's original insight: Whitman's mode, assimilationist rather than visionary, takes us along a path marked by comradeship-merging-death. [18] What does this have to do with the body, with the centrality of the body? We must be initially just a little more passive to Whitman, surrender ourselves a bit more than we have as critics to realize what this poetic mode enforces. Consider the familiar lines "I could turn and live with animals" [19] and "the look of the bay mare shames silliness out of me." [20] These lines might remind us of Wordsworth's "The Fountain,"

The blackbird amid leafy trees,
The lark above the hill,
Let loose their carols when they please,
Are quiet when they will.
With nature never do they wage
A foolish strife; they see
A happy youth and their old age
Is beautiful and free . . .

Wordsworth's next quatrain refers to the "heavy laws" which birds escape, laws which bind men. These are the very laws from which Whitman celebrated an imagined escape. The animals who in Rilke's eighth elegy look out beyond the enclosing circle of human preoccupations, who are unconstrained by memory, history, and the circle of their human loves, were conceived of as wholly alive till they die, as having lives of which death is a part.[21] Can men live such a life? In everyday terms this would be a life-and-death consciousness, momentaneous as a cat's, yet somehow aware, as Whitman put it, of "receiving identity through materials,"[22] aware of the "excrementitious body,"[23] as a leaf shed in death, having the axis of its existence not in memory but in the life of the body. Norman O. Brown has been at pains to characterize this state of consciousness in *Life Against Death*. If life in ordinary terms extends from self to family to community, this is life of another sort, felt as running from bodily identity to experienced assimilation and celebration of the world to a final assimilation: life identified with the upward thrust of the fountain (which in Wordsworth's poem is unceasing, is unchanged through many years of human experience), rather than with the linearity and finality of time and space and memory-bound existence.

I shall try in the next chapter to make plainer this disjunction between Wordsworth's sense of the bound character of our experience and Whitman's effort to find a mode for verse expressive of . . . what? Something we may provisionally call a consciousness at once momentaneous and aware of its commitment to the moment, like a cat with the imagination to apprehend its cathood. Our difficulty arises out of our critical tradition, which owes so much to the attitudes toward the poem and the image masterfully described in Frank Kermode's *Romantic Image* that we don't know where to set the Whitman I have described; we don't know whether what I have tried to describe is poetry or, alternatively, whether my description must be set aside because it doesn't refer to poetry based on the image.

And if it is not based on the image, am I therefore saying that it is based on "discourse"—for this is the alternative in the tradition Kermode has given a historical position? I should answer that there is another tradition which my references to Rilke are meant to call up; that it is not necessarily newer or better but that it has a different relation to discourse and to our sense of our humanity. We cannot say of Whitman that he wrote poems which must be admitted not to mean but to be. In an essay such as this I cannot dispose of the complex question raised by the relation between the implied makers and readers of such poems and the implied makers and readers of such poems as Whitman wrote. But I must attempt to sketch these last because I shall otherwise leave Whitman unrelated to his American readers and the history of the development of his mode in this country.

At the end of *Romantic Image*, published in 1957, Kermode suggests that the age which found the notion of the dissociation of sensibility a necessity must soon end; now it has ended, and this makes it easier to talk about Whitman.[24] Concomitant with the notion of and the achievement of the image was the cost in alienation from day-to-day concerns, from the heart and time-bound life. What must first be admitted about Whitman is that his mode was in one sense more, in another less, cut off from day-to-day concerns: more because the struggle to make poems, Yeats's quarrel with the self which was that of Irishman, Protestant, lover of women, amateur of magic, reader of Blake, was never undertaken by Whitman, whose "quarrel" was with a world precisely composed of such pluralities, all of which had to be subdued to the dream. And less, because Whitman was all along subject to consciousness, because he was the bard of a new consciousness which could never find release in images, but only in a delight in its own quality, yet remains always at the mercy of the moment. His novelty lay in his mode of apprehending the world, not in his success in winning timeless images from it. Hence, he is tied to such religous and quasi-religious figures as the elder James, Norman O. Brown, and Henry Miller. The image was not an axiological good for him; art was very nearly a crutch for him, to use Henry Miller's convenient extrapolation of this idea; the unliving of our bodily and cultural set was the primary imaginative task for Whitman, and he has finally little to do with the religion of art as we have tacitly developed it. I repeat, Whitman's terminus was not in images, in the life-in-death, death-in-life finality of images, but in a state of consciousness which my references to Wordsworth's fountain, to an aware cat, to Whitman's pervasive dream, are meant to suggest. To deal with him is to be continuously aware that he was both in and out of the game, that he is to be studied as a figure in the culture before whom existent critical vocabularies fail of application. That this is also true of Henry James, who was also in the end the proponent of a state of consciousness rather than a maker of images or an explorer of social reality, is a proposition that has encountered more resistance. I turn to it in the fifth chapter. Before I conclude this one, I wish to make some further suggestions about the qualities of Whitman's writing and the cultural place he made for himself.

I have called Whitman the poet of uncreation, of lapsing away, who sought to unlive the bodily habit social expectation had imposed. The other side of this undertaking is celebration of the momentaneous life-and-death experience. But a further attempt to suggest how his poetry is related to the palace of flesh, and to list the things it cancels out, will be useful. The cancellations are extensive. The world implied by the poetry is not one in which single words or persons or objects are discriminated, grasped, presented. Compare "I Saw in Louisiana a Live Oak Growing" with Wordsworth's "Tree, of many, one" [25] or Yeats's "great rooted blossomer." [26] It is not a world qualified by historical time or the perspectives of individual experience. It has no moments of dramatic significance which involve other figures. It has no terminal joys, no ac-

tions which may be defined as victories or defeats. Life is
not an affair of growth, or of the transcendence of prior
states. In this world suggested by the poetry, the responsive, the antiphonal, the other is absent. There are no
edges, no fringes, no symbols of the sort which, perceived
in momentary isolation, carry a penumbra of implication.
In it travel is as unimaginable as growth. The lighting of
a scene does not imply the possibility of other scenes. We
may take pleasure in associating Whitman with W. S.
Mount or Eakins, but the pleasure is ours. In Whitman
appearances fatally framed by light and shade undergo
dissolution. They submit to a vision of process and become
amenable to assimilation, to "the greed that with perfect
complaisance devours all things." [27] Yet this list of negatives must not be taken to imply that there is anything inherently factitious about the imaginative work that is
Whitman's poetry; it is an activity quite distinct from the
making of images, but no less a part of the world of
human possibility for that. We must be very much on our
guard against such gross appetites for imaginative order
as Northrop Frye's, who urges us to the making of an
"iconography of the imagination." [28] The imagination has
no metaphysically or even linguistically grounded tie to
icons alone. And as Kermode points out in *The Sense of an
Ending*, Frye's view of art may well lead to a transformation of all the things made by the imagination into a poten-
tially tyrannical myth. [29]

Our awareness of the differences it makes to live in various ways in our bodies is in some ways acute, in many
others spotty or misleading. Most of our perceptions of
this sort are hardly voiced. Whitman's is a case in which

more is asked of our sense of this matter than it is easy to give. For those who, like certain figures of the 1920's (or those who are at the moment seeking a felt disaffiliation from what they believe to be constraining forms of dress, clothing, sexuality, and speech), the body must bear more of the weight of assertion than it does for a bank clerk or even a professional basketball player, whose movements are after all consummated in numerical scores. Whitman's realization of the demands he was making on his little palace of flesh were profound and sure. That embryon of post-social man, Allen Ginsberg, one of Whitman's cultural descendants, recognizes such things with great accuracy, and carries the Whitman enterprise forward in the mode of Oriental body mysticism.

It is in particular the movements of his body, and the registration of its relation to the movements of other bodies, that Whitman's poetry seems best fitted to realize. He saw that he must come to feel his own body as a whole, altogether unqualified by social attitudes toward its parts and their functions. His insistence on the cleanliness and freshness of the body, anus and all, is part of an imaginative effort to create in others the belief he was seeking to enact and write down, the belief that the body and its relation to its world must be experienced integrally, felt to be as undivided from itself as a pollinating flower. That he did not wholly realize this, that there was an element of stagy exhibitionism in the beard, the open collar, the assumption of the bluffness, the boasting, is hardly surprising. But the poems, at least the best of them, are quite successful exhibitionism. This is no adolescent Rousseau lurking in an alley to show his penis, but in the best work a penis splendidly shown, a body "published," to use Emerson's term.

If this once more sounds like unqualified narcissism, I have misled the reader. I said earlier that Whitman communicated his delight in his body, and must now come back to the question of the audience, and the ways in which Whitman's emotional stance toward his own body and its *umwelt*, its ambience, generates an experiential space about it. If, for contrast, we take the phrase in Keats's letter, "The creature hath a purpose and its eye is bright with it," we find it easy to distinguish, just as we do when we find Keats writing, "the commonest man shows a grace in his quarrel." [30] This is the transitive mode, in which one moves toward ends and encounters others who hinder, aid, provoke a fresh recognition. It is not simply the world of action, since a poet such as Keats may be profoundly involved in it and find it the ground of poetry itself. For Whitman, we may be sure, this kind of generosity toward other existences was an impossibility. He could not make this concession to the plurality of things or to possibility. His chief imaginative task in the world was to envision it as an extension of himself and to provoke his pleasure in himself in others. In the business of writing, this latter impulse was primary. He could not simply celebrate self-discovery any more than Emerson could simply exploit his sense of private infinitude. How could he proclaim himself without destroying the authority of the sense of themselves in his readers? The vertical, the fountainlike thrust of self-assertion must be made a common experience. It was not simply the logical question of democratic idealism: How can we all be infinite without denying each other's being?

That question Emerson had not so much solved as worked with, accepted as a standing anomaly. But to experience one's own fullness, to be wholly seated in one's own imperium while affirming that of others, meant making a new language to conform to the intransitive character of what was to be communicated. Verbs of touching, fusing, flowing, a variety of attempts to find a language of process are the result. The implied Aristotelian world of kinds and logical ordering must be reshaped. The youth culture of the moment is trying for a concomitant reshaping of attitudes toward the body and language, and it affords illustrations of the meaning of Whitman's activity in the field of culture which were not available earlier.

I have emphasized what Whitman's poetry canceled out not in order to deny him a full quantum of humanity, but to try to suggest the force with which what he affirmed operated in the experiential field thus simplified or edited. For example, what has happened to Emerson's "nature," that grand phantasmagoria which is the theater of our discrimination of the correspondent orders of natural fact and spiritual fact? It has collapsed in Whitman into a landscape comprised of the body and its powers. F. O. Matthiessen's appetite for the pictorial in Whitman, which leads him to emphasize "landscapes projected masculine, full-sized golden," [31] an image associated with triumphant masturbation in "Song of Myself," is a good instance of the desperation with which criticism has attempted to supply pictures and discriminations, a visual field for judgment in a poet for whom the pictorial is simply unresolved material and is peripheral. Just as in Blake and the elder Henry James, Whitman's most profound sense of all existence was as the vehicle of a life identical with that he lived in his moments of fullest awareness. No such category as *nature* or *mineral* was allowed to stand in the way of this thrust toward assimilation. Nature, we may say, had no separate existence for Whitman (separate, that is, from serving, having served, or being about to serve as body to us all).

This chapter has dealt with Whitman largely from without as a figure in the culture; in the following chapter I analyze a single poem which is at once an independent whole and the most extraordinary of all representations of the assumption of an imperial self. Nowhere in Emerson can we find so full an acknowledgment that his wide claims were founded on an initial difficulty, the threat of personal disaster. Whitman filled in what is missing in Emerson's testimony.

Chapter IV

The World in the Body

Those who write about Whitman have lately tended to become partisans of one of the first three editions of *Leaves of Grass* (1855, 1856, 1860). The Whitman I am trying to describe is most clearly exhibited in the edition of 1856. I share Thoreau's conviction about this form of the work: the best things in it are "Song of Myself" (from 1855) and "Sun-Down Poem" (later called "Crossing Brooklyn Ferry"), which first appeared in 1856. (For the sake of convenient reference, "Crossing Brooklyn Ferry" has been printed as an appendix to this book on pages 247–54). The growth of this last poem may in part be traced in Whitman's notebook for 1855–6. Both "Crossing Brooklyn Ferry" and "Song of Myself" soften or dispel the megalomanic insistence of the 1855 Preface, in which we find all the rivers flowing into the great poet just as much as into the oceans, and the continent bounded just as much by the poet as by its coasts. The two poems escape that insistence in distinct ways. "Song of Myself" does so by creating a multiple cast of selves which flower out of one another and appear to incorporate one another; "Sun-Down Poem" does so by sinking the "I" in the recorded experience, and making the tremendous inversions and shifts of perspective the poem demands happen in the poem itself. The agent within the poem is the agent of these changes in us. They are referred to in an 1860 poem, "Whoever You Are Holding Me Now in Hand," as amounting to a complete disorientation and reorientation. (I should note that in what follows I confine myself to the poems of the 1855 and 1856 editions, chiefly in the form they finally assumed.)

In "Crossing Brooklyn Ferry" there is no reference to the poet as such. The eighth section announces the consummation of a union with the reader, who appears to have assumed the literally inexpressible powers of the poem's agent. The 1856 edition has a line which Whitman subsequently dropped:

> *What the push of reading could not start, is started*
> *by me personally, is it not?*

This recalls a line which appears in the 1855 edition (p. 57):

> *I pass so poorly with paper and types. . . . I must pass*
> *with the contact of bodies and souls.*

This assertion of an agency more inclusive and unmediated than print is something I must come back to, since

"Crossing Brooklyn Ferry" is in fact more successful in offering us an apprehended world than any other Whitman poem. The assertion of a power that dissolves the world of objects is made with a special urgency and force in the Whitman poem, which also gives us a stronger sense of objects than any other.

If it be admitted that this is the Whitman work most generous in its recognition of the immediacies of a physical world, we must at once add that it is the most terrifyingly successful in canceling them out or, rather, absorbing them into the imperial self. But there is more. The poem has the signal advantage for my essay—and for the expositor of Whitman—of explicitly characterizing the bad, the rejected, consequences of assuming that one plays a particular role or is defined by particular loves or hates. What the poem dissolves into the plenum of consciousness is not only the apprehended world, but the conventional epistemology, the way the world is beheld when it is conceived as the scene of drama and change, when it is conceived as determined by the way in which it is variously viewed by a man, a woman, a citizen, a child, in short, conceived by those who accept their identities and the relations they entail with others as fatal. The terminus toward which the poem moves is that of *The Golden Bowl*, although James offers us an image of the androgynous divine man and Whitman deals simply with the conditions necessary to his coming into being. This final man is shaped for us when Maggie Verver, at the end of *The Golden Bowl*, takes possession of her Prince and thus realizes the "body of humanity stretched out in time and space." [1] The terminus of the poem and that of the novel is emotionally and metaphysically the same. All persons assume universality—as Whitman has it, "What gods can exceed these that clasp me by the hand?"—and all objects, the "dumb beautiful ministers" of Whitman's poem, are appropriated as they are in Adam Verver's museum; as Whitman puts it, "we plant you permanently within us." In these works consciousness *becomes* unitary.

In this poem the bullying persona of the poet is absent; this is the distinction I emphasize in the preceding sentence. When the poet is present, the whole question of the struggle to attain his all-inclusive consciousness is ignored; he simply has it and invites the reader to enjoy it. In "Crossing Brooklyn Ferry" he tells the reader that he had shared his immersion in the mire and fury of the divided selves, but is now free, and he invites us to join him not simply through his fiat but through an explicit recognition of our common human fix:

> *I too knitted the old knot of contrariety* . . .

The agent of the poem is a person who "infuses" a fresh consciousness in us. After the fourth of the nine sections of the poem the verbs change, and the writer is no longer in the poem's present tense; he has taken on a species of timelessness the character of which is the very thing he wishes to convey. It is after this "death" that he asks whether he has succeeded in fusing his meaning into the person with whom he is trying to communicate.

This is the only Whitman poem in which the movement from one form of consciousness to another is operative within the poem; is in fact the structural hinge of the poem itself. The acknowledgment of a different way of viewing the world is not, of course, so generous as that of Henry James, whose magnificent Prince and supremely "social" Charlotte are representative of that consciousness which in Whitman is reduced to the "knot of contrariety." Yet everything in the poem does turn on the remarkable sixth section in which this line appears, and the writer's own freedom to assume the stance from which he triumphantly concludes has been won by overcoming the limitations posited in that sixth section.

In Whitman's work in general, the references to a posited resistance tend to be scattered and scornful and not, as they are here, an essential structural element. What Whitman contends with is familiar to his readers; he aims at the imaginative dissolution of every conceivable discrimination based on social, sexual, or generational role. It does not matter that you are the President, and if you think it does Whitman assures you that you won't understand him. We are not, as I put it in the preceding chapter, any more bound to one person than to another. If you are "curious" about God rather than your fellows, if you erect heaven and hell into realms distinct from the experienced world, you are numb to the actual seat of glory which is this world. As in Emerson, it is the Christian ethos which Whitman is fundamentally opposed to, or, to broaden it as we inevitably do, the basis of western character structure represented by the demands of parental figures and of conscience. The use of the term "evil" in the sixth section of "Crossing Brooklyn Ferry" points to this, and the past tense indicates the supersession of the whole personality based on internalized demands or guilt.

Discussion of Whitman ordinarily reads this demand

for change in the personality outward in the direction of "democracy" and individualism. What we must see is that Whitman is asking for an inward reconstitution of the self which will free it of guilt as a direct consequence of the imaginative undoing of the "knot of contrariety." He who

> *Blabb'd, blush'd, resented, lied, stole, grudg'd,*
> *Had guile, anger, lust, hot wishes I dared not speak,*
> (*Section 6, Lines 8–9*)

was dependent for his sense of himself on an internal dialectic, and on other persons who made claims on him or on whom he sought to make claims, and felt, as we are also told, inadequate, doubtful of his powers, guilty about masturbating, and so forth. To give up this dialectic of the emotions is to make a declaration of emotional independence which is the necessary complement of Emerson's declaration of intellectual independence. It is to assert that nobody depends on anybody else; that emotionally we pull ourselves up by our own bootstraps.

I have been insistent about the gain to the poem which results from Whitman's avoidance of an initial assertion that the "I" of the poem is a great poet. The paradoxical fact is that I must go on to describe an assumption of authority in the poem more complete, more like that of a god, than we can find consistently rendered anywhere else. I say "consistently" because this authority is established in a complete structure akin to that of dream or myth, and does not appear as the tag ends of a delusional system, as it does in the 1855 Preface. The elements are the same as those of the Preface and many of the poems of the first two editions, but here they are ordered within the form of the poem. When we associate this fact with what I have said about the poem's full-handedness, its rendering of sights, shapes, and movements, we begin to point to what it may be hard to overpraise: a genius which in the measure that it accepts has the power to transform the significance we attach to what it accepts, that is, the harbor, the gulls, the passengers, the sunset, the whole presented scene.

I must make one further point about Whitman's rejection of the role of poet in this particular poem. That role always involves him in a difficulty which arises not simply out of his claiming a special and inclusive authority, but also out of the implication that it will take time to realize that authority. The nature of the imputed authority in the "Ferry" poem is such that it cannot survive immersion in any temporal process; such temporal expressions as the poem uses must be subordinated to an eternity which is the present moment, and poets are too fatally associated with the notion of being read, and achieving their dominion over the imaginations of others in the course of time, to represent directly the underlying myth we are about to describe. To put it another way, the event of the poem is an apocalyptic event, and is brought about by an agent whose power to transform our consciousness goes beyond words because it is a power to transform the ways in which we apprehend words as well as the river or the sunset. (The fact that this event and the work of this agent appear in a poem is a triumph I will try to describe below.)

The agent with whom we have to deal in "Crossing Brooklyn Ferry" might provisionally be called a shaman; he has more in common with the practitioners of magic than with a publicly proclaimed poet. A shaman's powers are commensurate with natural powers; he uses words to lay hold of and transform persons and things. The Whitman who wrote this poem projected himself into it as shaman, and the account of the event in the poem has the kind of structure we associate with myth, in which shamans appear, or dream, which of course involves an imagined dreamer. Whether we turn to Lévi-Strauss or to Freud, we are assured that one doesn't finish examining such things as myths or dreams; exhaustive description of such structures ends by involving the whole universe from which they come. This is a warning that I can handle only prominent elements of the myth within this poem; I cannot, in this chapter, finish with something that actually extends to the whole of that pervasive dream which is behind Whitman's work.

The first such element I wish to bring out may be seen in relative isolation in a lesser Whitman poem, "A Song for Occupations."

All architecture is what you do to it when you look upon
it,
(Did you think it was in the white or gray stone? or the
lines of the arches and cornices?)

All music is what awakes from you when you are
reminded by the instruments . . .

(Section 4)

Will the whole come back then?
Can each see signs of the best by a look in the
looking-glass? is there nothing greater or more?
Does all sit there with you, with the mystic unseen soul?

Strange and hard the paradox true I give,
Objects gross and the unseen soul are one.

(*Section 5*)

When the psalm sings instead of the singer,
When the script preaches instead of the preacher . . .

When the minted gold in the vault smiles like the
night-watchman's daughter,
When warrantee deeds loafe in chairs opposite and are
my friendly companions,
I intend to reach them my hand, and make as much of
them as I do of men and women like you.

(*Section 6*)

The fourth through the eighth of these quoted lines parallel a number of things in the "Ferry" poem. But before I come to these, I paraphrase the most direct assertion of the quotation as a whole, that is, that bodies and images are simply correlative with "soul." They exist only in that they are apprehended; we exist only in the measure that we apprehend them. This is not the fully developed Blakean thesis that all things have their genesis in imagination; it is an assertion that what is seen is correlative with a seer or seers. If there is a power such that it institutes a fresh mode of seeing for somebody, that mode will not, either in this poem or in "Crossing Brooklyn Ferry," transcend the objects there produced for us. In sum, there is no evidence that in the Whitman of 1856 there is a separate realm in which "soul" enjoys an existence independent of a presented scene. We will see in a moment why this is so: the presented scene is totally inclusive. Meanwhile, I go back to the five lines from "A Song for Occupations" which afford a conveniently concise rendering of some of the themes of the "Ferry" poem.

The fourth line, "Will the whole come back then?", is a general reference to what is detailed in "Crossing Brooklyn Ferry," a total possession of all the images and objects and movements, all of which are apprehended by a "being than which none else is perhaps more spiritual," a rather lumpish designation of human beings who, earlier in the "Ferry" poem, are spoken of as those whom no imaginable gods could "exceed." It is a crucial point that when one considers the "whole" in "A Song for Occupations" (including, in the lines I have quoted, architecture, music, substances like gold, documents, and all they imply), one is looking at a variety of appearances which are all included in one's own image. The use of the image in the mirror as all-inclusive recalls the opening lines of "Crossing Brooklyn Ferry":

> *Flood-tide below me! I see you face to face!*
> *Clouds of the west—sun there half an hour high—I see*
> *   you also face to face.*

This invocation of a vast spectacle is anthropomorphically qualified by the word "face." The resonance with "A Song for Occupations" is with the "objects gross" which are one with the "unseen soul," and with the notion that the "whole" is mirrored if one looks in the glass. "Crossing Brooklyn Ferry" renders the "objects gross" as the "dumb beautiful ministers," and the 1855 Preface refers to them as "dumb real objects." Finally, as we shall see later, things seen become, at a rather terrifying level of generality, the "necessary film." At this point it is sufficient to remark that what we need is a way of defining the kind of imagined space in which we find ourselves. One thing about it is pretty clear. If "soul" is indeed correlative with appearance, the objects of any moment, if apprehended with the "free sense" referred to in the ninth section of "Crossing Brooklyn Ferry," will define eternity as well as those of any other moment.[2] My students have repeatedly wondered over the fact that the scene of the harbor described in the poem is presumed to persist unchanged; this is the result of the assertion that body and soul, image and beholder, are correlative. If they truly are, then eternity is what you truly see now, not what you hope for, remember, or try to imagine.

I must carry further the analysis of the use of images in the water, and the terms "identity" and "role" as they are employed in the poem. The last is qualified in three rather puzzling lines which need a gloss:

> *Play'd the part that still looks back on the actor or*
> *actress,*
> *The same old role, the role that is what we make it, as*
> *great as we like,*
> *Or as small as we like, or both great and small.*
>
> *(Section 6)*

My gloss comes from the second section of "A Song of the Rolling Earth":

> *The oration is to the orator, the acting is to the actor and*
> *actress not to the audience,*
> *And no man understands any greatness or goodness but*
> *his own, or the indication of his own.*

In the 1855 Preface Whitman wrote that all that is "well thought or done" remains attached to the "identities" from which the thoughts or actions spring. But what is of more importance here is the belief that we communicate nothing whatever by playing any specific role in the eyes of others. Life is not a story or a play; action with, for, or against others, relations of conflict or of reconciliation, realize nothing. In the 1855 Preface we find that the poet "sees eternity less like a play with a prologue and denouement . . . he sees eternity in men and women." The emotional logic is plain: no meaning is communicated through the wearing of a particular mask or participating in a dramatic action, for the action would then limit your expansion to the stature of a god who embraces the whole without selection or prejudice.

It may be objected that in "Song of Myself" the poet, the all-embracing subject, presents himself in various guises, makes what were called "pseudopodial" extensions, and returns upon himself in the previous chapter. We find him saying in the thirty-eighth section,

> *I find myself on the verge of a usual mistake.*

The mistake is defined for us a few lines below; it is not that of entering into the emotional ambience of others, but doing so in a fashion which betrays his supremacy by pinning him to a role:

> *That I could look with a separate look on my own crucifixion and bloody crowning!*

The danger of the "separate look" is precisely the danger that Emerson saw in historical Christianity, which Whit-

man, with customary audacity, has here employed as an
instance. To make this particular story crucial, to elevate a
particular personage into the only divinity, to be "curious"
about God, is to deny what Whitman reasserts at the end
of the thirty-eighth section, the connection between the infinite possibilities of a single man, and those of all the rest
of the potential gods or "unnumbered Supremes." [3] He enforces this by carrying forward the process of universaliz-
ing the Christ story and the resurrection; the grave opens
and

> *I troop forth replenish'd with supreme power, one of an
> average unending procession . . .*

But the gaiety and panache of "Song of Myself" is not
unmingled with terror; there is more to the business of
being an "identity" than simply making the assertion that
there are "unnumbered Supremes." The kind of imagined
space in which Whitman is to be found embraces extremes
of passivity and activity, which may be illustrated by some
further quotations. The first two suggest a spectrum of
kinds of relation to other identities. I quote first from "I
Sing the Body Electric," and then from "The Song of the
Answerer":

> *I have perceived that to be with those I like is enough,*
> *To stop in company with the rest at evening is enough,*
> *To be surrounded by beautiful, curious, breathing*
> *   laughing flesh is enough,*
> *To pass among them or touch any one or rest my arm*
> *   ever so lightly round his or her neck for a*
> *   moment, what is this then?*
> *I do not ask any more delight, I swim in it as in a sea.*

> *There is something in staying close to men and women,
> and looking on them, and in the contact and odor
> of them, that pleases the soul well,*
> *All things please the soul but these please the soul well.*
>
> > *(Section 4)*
>
> *Him all wait for, him all yield up to, his word is decisive
> and final,*
> *Him they accept, in him lave, in him perceive themselves
> as amid light,*
> *Him they immerse and he immerses them.*
>
> > *(Section 1)*

The first quotation, from the fourth section of "I Sing the
Body Electric," gives us but one half the pattern that
emerges in the second from the "Answerer" in which the
eponymous figure is both immersed and immersing. These
two passages may stand as instances of these posited extremities. We will encounter the light-giver in whom
others perceive themselves below. In "Crossing Brooklyn
Ferry" these extremes emerge as parts of a discernible
structure in which the maker of the poem occupies both
extremes simultaneously. I shall call it, a little arbitrarily,
the "complex of centrality." John Kinnaird, in a brilliant
essay originally published in 1958, establishes a context
for this discussion.[4] Writing about the 1855 volume, he
says, "If, however, we read the poetry with an uncom-
mitted eye, we find that we are never really in a consciously American world, but always within the purely
magical universe of Whitman's 'self' and its strange visi-
tations." [5] Kinnaird shares the view expressed in the previous chapter that for Whitman the repossession of the
body is axial, and connects it to admirable effect with the
paradox of democratic idealism, familiar as Emerson's

claim that each self concenters all the rays of universal being yet does not "countervail," to use Whitman's term, any other identity. He justly says that the paradox of this sort of identity is richer in Whitman than in Emerson. He feels, again rightly, that Whitman commentators have erred in failing to disentangle the "magical universe" from the assertiveness of the boastful American bard. But he doesn't quite see how much the bard is entangled in the "magical universe" and misses the indispensable documentation of the qualities of the latter in the 1855 Preface.

As readers of Whitman, we have oftenest failed for the reason endemic in the new critical period; we didn't take his humanity any more seriously than we took our own— our critical terms didn't reckon with our humanity—and our attention to Whitman has been governed by the largely unconscious denials and the largely unconscious slovenliness which marked our own attitudes toward the emotional uses we found for literature. Leslie Fiedler has always sought to avoid the traps of closed universes of critical discourse; we find him saying that Whitman's personal life was a disaster, but he doesn't go on to relate the disaster to the triumph; Whitman-the-man-in-a-fix has been excluded from his poetry.[6] This leaves the field open for such aseptically professional statements as this one of Paul Fussell's, which has to do with "Out of the Cradle Endlessly Rocking": "The 'key' which the boy seeks and finds in the poem will not, I think, admit us into any of the dark, winding corridors of Whitman's actual life. But the key does do something even better. It unlocks both for Whitman and for us the front door of the palace of art."[7] In other words, no matter what sort of affirmation or denial of the qualities of life is being made in this poem, we are home free in the sacred realm.

But there is no longer much point in fussing about the inhumanity of criticism to writers, or about the failure to assume a discriminable moral and cultural responsibility that it involved. The young, the professor's clients, have breached the sacred realm; they are interested in the quality of life, in consciousness, and we may be sure that the professors will follow meekly enough. Art has once more become a handmaiden.

If it is indeed consciousness with which we are once more involved, we find ourselves back where the serious discussion of American literature began, in D. H. Lawrence's *Studies in Classic American Literature*. Lawrence's challenge runs in effect: What sort of consciousness defines the American? The young do not share his interest or mine in the genesis of cultural attitudes in time. But those who do will be willing to consider my view that Whitman has had cultural descendants who amply confirm Lawrence's thesis that the important thing to discover was the quality of life that the poet had envisaged. Henry Miller, Norman O. Brown, and Allen Ginsberg won't allow us to forget that the cultural space emptied out in Whitman's imagination, that whole James Russell Lowell world in which he found it impossible to live, was indeed filled by something, filled, let us say, by what Kinnaird calls his "magical universe."

When we find Whitman saying in the 1855 Preface that the world is properly grasped only in the sensorium of the greatest poet, we have been in the habit of labeling the fact "Whitman" and making no more of it. But a modicum

of sympathy would lead us to acknowledge that that assertion, and indeed the tone of the whole Preface, is that of a
man terribly beset. Again, we are using Whitman for our
purposes and failing to recall his kinship with us as a man.
One reason for our blindness is that, beginning in the
1950's, Whitman enjoyed a great triumph among us. But
the fact that in the 1950's the world of differentiated social
and sexual role was cracking, slipping, and fading away at
an accelerated rate was the condition of that triumph. We
had begun to occupy something like Whitman's psychic
space, and for the first time we found ourselves at home
with his poetry. But what we are now considering is the
initial condition, not the delayed public result one hundred
years later. Such a total assertion of self-sufficiency as is
made in the 1855 Preface is the final refuge of a consciousness which has absolutely no assured claim on anyone else.
(This complements the statement of the last chapter, that
Whitman's presumption was that he was no more bound
to any one person than another.)

These two lines from the crucial sixth section of "Crossing Brooklyn Ferry"

> *Saw many I loved in the street or ferry-boat or public*
> *assembly, yet never told them a word,*
> *Lived the same life with the rest, the same old laughing,*
> *gnawing, sleeping . . .*

are piteous, like a fist never unclenched. But it would be
naïve of us to say, "Why didn't he pick up his young men
if he wanted them so much?" We should be quarreling not
only with the conditions of his success as the poet of our
poem—of all his best work up through the 1856 volume—

but with what was its essential condition: that he be at once near and far, that he touch only lightly, that he be located not in the space in which a breathing lover stood, but within the psychic space of Kinnaird's "magical universe," which I propose to call the "complex of centrality." The putative lovers could not have broken through to him had they tried; his psychic demand outran what any or all of them could have supplied. He was a man in an agonizing fix, but instead of falling back on the utter solipsism of complete delusion, he faced about and carried his cosmic inward spectacle to the print-shop. The writer of these poems was an amazing man, a shaman without a tribe to follow him, who nonetheless believed that he could, by using words, communicate a sense of the world, a mode of consciousness, that would create a tribe for him—and turned out to be right! We may say that he was not only desperate but also mad if we like, but the point is that cultural innovation rests in this instance on exemplary madness, a distortion of self which entered into the history of our culture. I am not speaking simply of the kind of welcome Whitman's mode of consciousness began to get in the 1950's, but of the fact that the poems of 1855 and 1856 were written down then, a hundred years earlier, and have ever since been emitting that peculiar energy I find in "Crossing Brooklyn Ferry."

The remainder of my discussion aims at three things: showing how the myth or dream clustering about the complex of centrality figures in the poem; showing that the myth is confronted in the poem by the thing denied, that is, the emotional and cultural set of a dialectic, transitive world of social and sexual roles in which guilt is the defin-

ing characteristic, and trying to indicate the nature of the
ties between the myth and the poem in which it appears.
Meanwhile, we must keep in mind the fact that we are
dealing with work produced before Whitman apparently
did take a lover, and before he became inextricably tangled
with the consequences of the public response to *Leaves of
Grass*.[8] Our ur-Whitman had had Emerson's praise, but
he had not had a chance to develop a public role, nor become a public man. Kinnaird takes the position that the
best of his work is to be found in the 1855 volume; I prefer
to say the 1856 volume, if two or three of the poems of
1860 are included.

I begin my discussion of the complex of centrality with
these lines from "Who Learns My Lesson Complete":

> *It is no small matter, this round and delicious globe
>   moving so exactly in its orbit for ever and ever,
>   without one jolt or the untruth of a single
>   second . . .*
>
> <div align="right">(<i>Line 13</i>)</div>

> *Is it wonderful that I should be immortal? as every one
>   is immortal;
> I know it is wonderful, but my eyesight is equally
>   wonderful, and how I was conceived in my
>   mother's womb is equally wonderful,*

> *And pass'd from a babe in the creeping trance of a couple
>   of summers and winters to articulate and walk—
>   all this is equally wonderful.*
>
> <div align="right">(<i>Lines 19–21</i>)</div>

> *And that the moon spins round the earth and on with the
>   earth, equally wonderful,*

And that they balance themselves with the sun and stars
is equally wonderful.

(*Lines 25–6*)

The poem as a whole equates the process of Whitman's
growth and his widening awareness with the exquisite certainty of planetary motion. It is in this context that we
must learn to read the extraordinary sentence about the
poet in the 1855 Preface: "He judges not as the judge
judges, but as the sun falling around a helpless thing." I
quote two long passages from the Preface which fill out
our sense of the imagined relations between being in precisely the right place, or performing an exquisitely determined motion, with light, with eyesight, and the multiplicity of the centers of consciousness:

> The greatest poet hardly knows pettiness or triv-
> iality. If he breathes into any thing that was before
> thought small it dilates with the grandeur and life of
> the universe. He is a seer. . . . he is individual . . .
> he is complete in himself. . . . the others are as good
> as he, only he sees it and they do not. He is not one of
> the chorus. . . . he does not stop for any regulation
> . . . he is the president of regulation. What the eye-
> sight does to the rest he does to the rest. Who knows
> the curious mystery of the eyesight? The other senses
> corroborate themselves, but this is removed from any
> proof but its own and foreruns the identities of the
> spiritual world. A single glance of it mocks all the
> investigations of man and all the instruments and
> books of the earth and all reasoning. What is marvel-
> lous? what is unlikely? what is impossible or baseless

or vague? after you have once just opened the space of a peachpit and given audience to far and near and to the sunset and had all things enter with electric swiftness softly and duly and without confusion or jostling or jam.

The land and sea, the animals, fishes and birds, the sky of heaven and the orbs, the forests mountains and rivers, are not small themes . . . but folks expect of the poet to indicate more than the beauty and dignity which always attach to dumb real objects. . . . they expect him to indicate the path between reality and their souls.

And in a later passage,

The messages of great poets to each man and woman are, Come to us on equal terms, Only then can you understand us, We are no better than you, What we enclose you enclose, What we enjoy you may enjoy. Did you suppose there could be only one Supreme? We affirm there can be unnumbered Supremes, and that one does not countervail another any more than one eyesight countervails another . . . and that men can be good or grand only of the consciousness of their supremacy within them.

Just as in treating Emerson we were forced to accept the essential contradiction between a total receptivity, attaining a proper "sphericity" to focus all the rays of being and an assertion of supremacy which made the individual the final arbiter of the nature of reality, so here we must accept the double assertion that through being wholly passive, receiving all through the eye (which is associated with a "peachpit," a mythological symbol of the fundamental container, the vagina, no doubt, because of its shape and the character of its surface[9]) we become a "Supreme," all things become subject to us and the process assures us of our proper grandeur. But in Whitman the emotional character of this marriage of extremities becomes plainer to us than it was in Emerson. Whitman too makes abstract statements such as that the poet's sympathy is as measureless as his pride and that they "balance," but his work enables us to understand their function in ordering his personality without so much interpretive effort. I ought also to note that Whitman uses the laws of optics to attempt a resolution of the paradox of "unnumbered Supremes"; all cats may look at all kings, and every cat becomes equally a king in doing so. Each center subtends the whole. I employ the adage "a cat may look at a king" to suggest the stress looking bears; we shall discover later on that the overwhelming character of the thing we look at is beautifully articulated by Whitman.

Our notoriously loose and even sloppy poet found the idea of an ultimate precision imaginatively indispensable. The passages just now quoted from the Preface may have seemed mere rant to us. But for the man involved they were wholly necessitated, as inescapable as Rilke's "*Jeder engel ist schrecklich . . .*"[10] To treat Whitman as if he were real is to treat him as if his whole being was indeed involved in his best work. For him as well as for Rilke, beauty was edged with terror, and what I am describing as the complex of centrality matches the passivity at once

longed for and feared with an assertion of supreme power
—figures babe and god in one person.

I go on with my train of quotations. These lines are
from the sixteenth and seventeenth sections of "Song of
Myself":

> *I resist anything better than my own diversity*
> *Breathe the air but leave plenty after me,*
> *And am not stuck up and am in my place.*
>
> *(The moth and the fish eggs are in their place,*
> *The bright suns I see and the dark suns I cannot see are*
> *   in their place,*
> *The palpable is in its place and the impalpable is in its*
> *   place.)*
>
> *   (Lines 349-54)*
>
> *If they are not just as close as they are distant they are*
> *   nothing.*
>
> *   (Line 358)*

In the 1855 Preface we are told that in the work of the poet
there will be "nothing too close, nothing too far off." The
poet himself is "commensurate with a people," "equalizer
of his age and land," "arbiter of the diverse." He "scorns
intervals," he exhibits "precision and balance." In the
eighth section of "The Sleepers" he writes, "The universe
is duly in order, every thing is in its place . . ." What
happens when one is not in one's place? The sixth section
of "Crossing Brooklyn Ferry" suggests the dislocation
which follows from knowing what it is to be evil. In fact,
evil is really a name for being out of one's place, or, alternatively, playing the "small" role instead of the "great"

one. The 1855 Preface has it, "nothing out of its place is good and nothing in its place is bad."

My earlier quotations from "I Sing the Body Electric" and "The Song of the Answerer" led me to say that there is a kind of scale between immersing and being immersed, but we shall have to sophisticate that initial realization that Whitman is positing extremes, extremes which fall within Kinnaird's "magical universe" rather than the world of physically measured space. One can be out of one's "place" in one's own body, just as one may have a "castrated face," an epithet I take from the poem "Faces." The way in which you, so to speak, occupy your body, is involved. We had better speak, as Géza Róheim does, of libidinized space, something like a dream space in that it is built out of the body or felt to be an extension of the body.[11] For example, I turn to one of the most mysteriously powerful of passages in Whitman, which comes at the end of the twenty-fourth and the opening of the twenty-fifth sections of "Song of Myself":

> *To behold the daybreak!*
> *The little light fades the immense and diaphanous*
>   *shadows,*
> *The air tastes good to my palate.*
> *Hefts of the moving world at innocent gambols silently*
>   *rising, freshly exuding,*
> *Scooting obliquely high and low.*
>
> *Something I cannot see puts upward libidinous prongs,*
> *Seas of bright juice suffuse heaven.*
>
> *The earth by the sky staid with, the daily close of their*
>   *junction,*

The heav'd challenge from the east that moment over my
   head,
The mocking taunt, See then whether you shall be master!

25

Dazzling and tremendous how quickly the sun-rise would
   kill me,
If I could not now and always send sun-rise out of me.

We also ascend dazzling and tremendous as the sun,
We found our own O my soul in the calm and cool of the
   daybreak.

The solar character of the "soul," which also rises up or
awakens in the morning, is a familiar mythological motif.
We must make the imaginative concession; just as the sun
has also been endowed with desire and streams as a living
substance, so Whitman has been endowed with the power
and precision of planetary motion; both are in the same
imagined space.[12] Moreover, the primal power of that at
which we look is vividly established. The poet's fantasy of
centrality does not allow him to approach another person
too nearly, but this does not preclude a nicely measured
contention with the infant giant, the sun, born afresh of
the nightly junction of earth and sky. Here Whitman and
sun are twinned powers neither physical nor psychic, but
both at once. A marriage which counters that of the sky
and earth has been consummated between Whitman's soul
and the daybreak scene, or, more generally, the "dumb
beautiful ministers"; soul has married "the necessary
film," and the issue is light, the light that Whitman himself emits.

To illustrate Whitman's preoccupation with himself as light-bringer, I go back to the 1855 Preface, in which expressions related to vision and light occur: "what the eyesight does to the rest he does to the rest," and "high up out of reach he stands turning a concentrated light," as well as, "From the eyesight proceeds another eyesight." Additional expressions of the same preoccupation occur elsewhere in the Preface. "The greatest poet does not only dazzle his rays over character and scenes and passions . . . he exhibits the pinnacles that no man can tell what they are for or what is beyond . . . he glows a moment on the extremest verge." This recalls not simply the encounter with the sun in the twenty-fourth and twenty-fifth sections of "Song of Myself," but the opening of the "Ferry" poem, in which Whitman is "face to face" with the sun. The connection of his activity and this natural force is emphasized a little further on in the Preface, in the phrase "the sunshine of the light of letters." And the effort to create a context in which the effect of his words and that of the movement of these bodies emitting light may be measured is suggested by the assertion that the spectacle of the sun and moon journeying through the heavens does not give more "satisfaction" than the poet gives through his poetry. And lastly, there is a light upon light itself, "As they emit themselves facts are showered over with light. . . . the daylight is lit with more volatile light. . . . also the deep between the setting and the rising sun goes deeper many fold." The phrase "due emission," part of a passage cut from the end of the seventh section of the "Ferry" poem, suggests an imaginative binding of light and semen through the common verb "to emit" which I develop further below. At this stage I wish to emphasize the phallic suggestions of "the deep between the setting and the rising sun."

The invasion of darkness by light, and of light by darkness, sexually represented, is a commonplace in the writer who sees the great poet as the world's only "complete lover" in the 1855 Preface and in "Song of Myself." In "I Sing the Body Electric" we find the night invading day:

> Bridegroom night of love working surely and softly into
> the prostrate dawn,
> Undulating into the willing and yielding day,
> Lost in the cleave of the clasping and sweet-flesh'd day.
> (Lines 61–3)

I quote this passage as an instance of the fact that representations of sexual intercourse or seminal emission are generally cosmic in character; the "deep" between the setting and the rising sun in my quotation from the Preface awaits a penetrating light which has a phallic association. A reference to futurity in "Song of Myself" has the same extraordinary inflation; the poet puts himself to "the ambush'd womb of the shadows." We must bear in mind the extremities suggested above, a total submission, as in the fifth and the linked twenty-eighth and twenty-ninth sections, of "Song of Myself," and on the other side a gigantesque assertion of power figured through light and flood,[13] as in the address to the sea, "Dash me with amorous wet, I can repay you." [14] These are simply more specific forms of the antithesis between immersing and being immersed in "The Song of the Answerer" quoted above, which contains half of the complementary use of light, "in him perceive themselves as amid light." (We have already met a Whitman who fills out the pattern in the quotation from the twenty-fourth and twenty-fifth sections of "Song of Myself" in which the writer, a body defined by light from the sun, sends out a light which itself defines other bodies including the sun at daybreak.[15] The representation of this complementary relationship in the "Ferry" poem is discussed below.)

The reader may have noted a striking echo of Emerson's comparison of himself to a "transparent eyeball" in the passage quoted from the Preface above, in which Whitman speaks of all things as invading "the space of a peachpit." No term for a counter-assertion based on the body was available to Emerson. Whitman's gigantic extension of the powers of the phallus to emit semen or of the "face" to emit light is replaced in Emerson by the powers of "soul" or, more specifically, those of the "grand" ego. (Emerson, we ought to remind ourselves, felt the danger of loss of control in the situation; he speaks of himself as "glad to the brink of fear.") Despite Emerson's elision of the bodily term, the emotional situation is very much the same. Both men are pinned Gullivers, submitting to the totality of experience on the one side and titans filling all space on the other; the measure of submission dictates the measure of assertion. They are to be found on either side of the bustle of the society of reciprocal roles, the middle ground of life, on which we fall in love, change the diapers, call each other names, and are bounded by other people, as well as by nature and our reveries and dreams.

But "Crossing Brooklyn Ferry" reunites the passive and the supremely active halves, catches up the world within Whitman's extended body, catches up even the thing denied, those still bound by "the knot of contrariety." I must now attempt a description of the myth internal to the poem, and the sixth section in which we encounter the "knot," the myth dissolves.[16]

The nine sections of the poem run to one hundred thirty-two lines. It was originally published without these divisions. Whitman unquestionably improved on the poem in later editions. I shall employ the final text and refer to the 1856 version and the passages from the notebook of 1855–6 when these seem significant. In the first section the person whom I have denominated the "agent" sees "face to face" the flood-tide, the "sun there half an hour high," and the "clouds of the west," as well as the crowds of men and women returning home, who are "curious" to him "and more in my meditations" than they imagine, as are the future crossers of the ferry, "years hence." This opening reminds us, as I have noted, of the tremendous confrontation with the sun in "Song of Myself," but here Whitman is to appear not simply as the infinitely powerful agent who transforms the scene, but also as a part of the scene, a passenger on the ferry, a man who had been bound by guilt, a mortal man, and so forth. To register the final triumph of "soul," the poem orchestrates an extraordinarily diverse set of movements, movements conventionally of differing orders which are imaginatively assimilated into a single vision that abrogates temporal and logical distinctions. I won't pretend to list them all, but there are the movements of the ferry toward the Brooklyn shore, of the other vessels, of flapping pennants and of the flaring lights of the foundry chimneys, of the gulls, of the sun, of the precession of the equinoxes, of the flood-tide and the ebb-tide, of persons in the streets and of the passengers on the ferry who stand yet are "hurried," of human generations, past, present, and to come, of those tethered like bull-calves by the "knot of contrariety," that is, by such emotions as bind them, of "soul" itself, which attaches itself to the "necessary film" of appearance that envelops it.

This flux of movement amounts to a procession of life, a march of the generations for which Whitman has found a scene in the harbor, the cities on either side, the hills of Jersey, and the sunset. His aim as regisseur of this gigantic spectacle dictates his use of these movements and is consummated when, with "free sense"—no longer bound by "contrariety"—we are able to embrace the multiplicity of things and processes seen, "we plant you permanently within us."

The second section of the poem describes the agent as fed by all the things seen, as perishing, and at the same time living in an eternal moment,

> *The simple, compact, well-join'd scheme, myself*
> *   disintegrated every one disintegrated yet part of*
> *   the scheme,*
> *The similitudes of the past and those of the future,*
> *The glories strung like beads on my smallest sights and*
> *   hearings . . .*

He goes on to invoke the "others" with whom he will have a community of consciousness, thus democratizing a passage referring to the poet in the Preface which makes the link between eternity and the momentaneous more explicit.

In this passage the realization is reserved to the poet; in the poem it is at once shared.

> . . . and if he be not himself the age transfigured
> . . . and if to him is not opened the eternity which
> gives similitude to all periods and locations and proc-
> esses and animate and inanimate forms, and which is
> the bond of time, and rises up from its inconceivable
> vagueness and infiniteness in the swimming shape of
> today, and is held by the ductile anchors of life, and
> makes the present spot the passage from what was to
> what shall be, and commits itself to the representa-
> tion of this wave of an hour and this one of the sixty
> beautiful children of the wave—let him merge in the
> general run and wait his development . . .

Returning to the poem, I note that all will be subject to "disintegration," all will be equally fed by these sights. The third section opens with the line, "It avails not, time nor place—distance avails not . . ." In the 1856 edition two lines take a form which makes the agent's temporal omnipresence more explicit; he is in the past, the present, and the future. In the final version of the third section the second line runs, "I am with you, you men and women of a generation, or ever so many generations hence . . ." He goes on to say, using the past tense, that he felt as they do, or will; that he also was one of a crowd; he too "stood yet was hurried" by the movement of the "current." To be hurried by the "current" rather than simply by the move-ment of the ferry is an indication of a figurative current of life, and has something of the indefiniteness of the passage from the Preface in which we are held "by the ductile anchors of life." These shapes and appearances of the harbor, marvelously busy and animated for us in this third section, include the agent who "Look'd at the fine centrifugal spokes of light round the shape of my head in the sunlit water," and had had his "eyes dazzled by the shimmering track of beams." Out of this passivity to light and the scene will spring his emanation of light. Or I may borrow from the Preface, again with the restrictive reference to the poet which "Crossing Brooklyn Ferry" omits, "Other proportions of the reception of pleasure dwindle to nothing to his proportions." This receptiveness is to be universalized in the poem, in which we all gain Whitman's "free sense."

The fourth section enforces the identical nature of the agent's response to the scene with that of future crossers, and extends it logically: they will have the same power to look back on him as he has to look forward to them. (I noted above on page 130 that this power derives from their awareness of the totality of the scene, which is akin to Whitman's, and is not dependent on acting a particular "role" that relates them to the poem's agent.) What remains to be defined is the kind of apprehension of totality which permits the agent and all these others now and in the future to share a mode of self-possession through a common possession of the "necessary film." The process is what the four following sections, the fifth through the eighth, are about. (The ninth and last is a triumphant account of the whole process which assumes that those acted upon by our agent have indeed been infused by his meaning.) All four take place after the indication that the agent may stop for a day and a night but must inevitably be carried away by the current. The fourth section, then, ends with his "death." This puts increased stress on the reiteration that time, place, and distance "avail not" in the third line of the fifth section. The answer to the question "What is it then between us?" becomes wholly assured in the eighth section, when we are all gods together; the answer is that we then share totality. (This is the alternative to speaking to the young men whom Whitman "never told" a word; in this 1856 poem Whitman, to invert the emphasis in the direction of ordinary life, can *only* know us as gods, can only know everybody. To know particular persons is not in his power.)

For expository purposes it seems best to jump to the seventh and eighth sections, in which the agent's triumph is recorded, and then undertake an explanation of the fifth and sixth. (The ninth, splendid though it is, is simply a coda to the rest, and we need refer to it only as it amplifies what precedes it.)

The seventh section is short:

> *Closer yet I approach you,*
> *What thoughts you have of me now, I had as much of*
> *   you—I laid in my stores in advance,*
> *I consider'd long and seriously of you before you were*
> *   born.*
>
> *Who was to know what should come home to me?*
> *Who knows but I am enjoying this?*
> *Who knows for all the distance, but I am as good as*
> *   looking at you, for all you cannot see me?*

The reason time, distance, and place do not avail is that the shaman, agent, magician, ghost has satisfied the condition which fulfills "soul," makes "identity" or "role" "complete":

> *I swear the earth shall surely be complete to him or her*
> *who shall be complete.*
> *The earth remains jagged and broken only to him or her*
> *who remains jagged and broken.*
>
> *("A Song of the Rolling Earth," Lines 90–1)*

The poet has himself defined that condition as not susceptible of literal expression. It is of course externally indicated as the momentaneous life-and-death awareness I sought to describe in the last chapter. But we may now speak of it with somewhat more precision as a simultaneous realization of the extremes of activity and passivity, or as a realization of the complex of centrality—being in one's "place." Whitman tried, in these lines of the 1856 version of "Crossing Brooklyn Ferry," to instruct the reader, to demonstrate that any point in time could be universalized as a moment of awareness which enabled one to command the whole of being:

> *It is not you alone, nor I alone,*
> *Not a few races, not a few generations, not a few*
> *centuries,*
> *It is that each came, or comes, or shall come from its due*
> *emission, without fail, either now, or then, or*
> *henceforth,*
> *Everything indicates—the smallest does, and the largest*
> *does,*
> *A necessary film envelops all, and envelops the soul for*
> *the proper time.*

Whitman did not drop these lines until 1881, although they spoil the whole movement of the poem as we now have it by anticipating the generalization which catches up all sights and objects into the "necessary film" in the concluding section, and, more important still, they blur the assertion of the agency of our shaman in the eighth section by suggesting that his power can be rationalized with temporal expressions.

The omission of these lines creates an admirable progression from the seventh to the eighth sections. In the seventh our agent or shaman approaches us more nearly; in the eighth we learn that it is precisely by emitting his light or pouring out his semen that he brings about the relation of the total scene to those whom he is addressing:

> *What gods can exceed these that clasp me by the hand,*
> *and with voices I love call me promptly and*
> *loudly by my nighest name as I approach?*
> *What is more subtle than this which ties me to the woman*
> *or man that looks in my face? [light]*
> *Which fuses me into you now, and pours my meaning*
> *into you? [semen]*
>
> *We understand then do we not?*
> *What I promis'd without mentioning it, have you not*
> *accepted?*
> *What the study could not teach—what the preaching*
> *could not accomplish is accomplish'd, is it not?*

We are now in a position to say that "Crossing Brooklyn Ferry" carries forward what the "self" manages in sections twenty-four and twenty-five of the "Song of Myself." The marriage of Whitman's soul to the "calm and cool of daybreak," the contention in which he masters the sun, made him "complete." The eighth section of the "Ferry" poem shows him working his spell on us, marrying our souls to the "dumb, beautiful ministers," ultimately the "necessary film."

I noted in the last chapter that Whitman, both in and out of the game of literary criticism as we have been playing it, often simply escapes; our vocabularies don't lay hold of him. He has a design on us, is busy trying to alter our consciousness, and we are busy trying to cobble his esthetic objects into independent entities. The result is that, since the acute but outraged responses of Santayana[17] and John Jay Chapman,[18] who sensed what was going on and didn't like it, we have had very little comment on Whitman (always excepting D. H. Lawrence and those whom I have called his "cultural descendants") which is of much account. Yet "Crossing Brooklyn Ferry" *is* a poem, and the techniques of textual criticism are relevant to it; the difficulty cannot be solved until criticism has a vocabulary which acknowledges the humanity of the poet and the critic as well as the character of the object to be examined.

This poem demands the creation of such a critical context; in its absence I must improvise as I can. To revert to the infusion of the agent's meaning into us in the eighth section: the *pouring* of meaning is of course related to the figurative *immersion* of passages quoted earlier, and Whitman's habit of bringing together light and flood is an association of things with a common emotional root. Light, the face, the phallus, and an emission are in fact bound together. The genitalization of the face becomes explicit in the poem "Faces":

> *The face withdrawn of its good and bad . . . a castrated*
> *face.*
> *A wild hawk . . . his wings clipped by the clipper,*

*A stallion that yielded at last to the thongs and the knife
of the gelder.*

(Lines 11–13)

Again we must note a clinically dramatic contrast between
two attitudes toward *pouring* in the poem. In the 1856 version's sixth section we find among the list of human distortions and limitations a reference to the speaker as a "solitary committer," that is, a masturbator. The juxtaposition
of this with the triumphant pouring of the eighth section
suggests that emitting semen and light are assimilated to
utterance, the effect of utterance. We have a kind of
wholly triumphant, wholly guiltless orgasm.

Before turning to the most direct expression of the myth
or complex of centrality, I note certain other details which
have the stamp of dream material. The ferry is entered
through gates, and moves from "mast-hemm'd Manhattan," carrying its hundreds of passengers *toward* the
"ample hills" of Brooklyn. When this is reiterated in the
ninth section it becomes

*Stand up tall masts of Mannahatta! stand, beautiful hills
of Brooklyn!*

(Line 105)

This movement of the passengers on the ferry suggests
uterine or thalassal regression, but the latter emphasis is
clearest in a second movement, which carries the passengers out to sea on the "current," a motif familiar from
"Out of the Cradle Endlessly Rocking." (We must recall
that our agent undergoes a "death.") The suggestion of a
primal scene in the movement of the ferry is reduplicated
in the line describing the foundry chimneys,

> *Casting their flicker of black contrasted with wild red and*
>   *yellow light over the tops of the houses and down*
>   *into the clefts of streets* . . .
>
> (*Section 3, Line 48*)

It recurs once more in the flight, a dream constant for phallic activity, of the oscillating gulls. These remarkable gulls deserve a little space. They make one think twice about an apparently innocent piece of bombast in the Preface: "if he [the poet] breathes into anything that was before thought small it dilates with the grandeur and life of the universe." Our negligently leaning idler on the ferry

> *Watched the Twelfth-month sea-gulls, saw them high in*
>   *the air floating with motionless wings, oscillating*
>   *their bodies,*
> *Saw how the glistening yellow lit up parts of their bodies*
>   *and left the rest in strong shadow,*
> *Saw the slow-wheeling circles and the gradual edging*
>   *toward the south,*
> *Saw the reflection of the summer sky in the water* . . .
>
> (*Section 3, Lines 28–31*)

These are December gulls, whose "edging" toward the south in "slow-wheeling circles" images the winter solstice and the death of the year—and the very next line lands us plump in summer! The lounger has compassed a year in an instant of vision which abrogates time, and the association gull/flight/sun comes forward to reinforce the sun/light/phallus association in the context of "oscillating" movement.[19]

But these are accessory details. I go on to the complex of centrality illustrated above from the Preface and from other poems. It is indeed connected with one aspect of dreams. To sink into a dream is plausibly interpreted as entering into the libidinized space of one's own body, living in the universe as if it were your body—this is a kind of literary commonplace. We find Borges quoting Addison, "When the soul dreams [he writes] it is the theater, the actors and the audience." The agent of our poem is both the scene and the light which reveals it in the poem. Whn all things enter "the space of a peachpit" without "confusion or jostle or jam," the passive-active extremities are reduplicated: submitting to light, Whitman masters the light by emitting a light beyond light, is once again, or at the same time, active.

The lines I now quote are from the end of the fifth section, which opens with "What is it then between us?"

> *I too had been struck from the float forever held in*
> *solution,*
> *I too had receiv'd identity by my body,*
> *That I was I knew was of my body, and what I should be*
> *I knew I should be of my body.*

Whitman uses "float" on occasion in a sense akin to Aristotle's *prima materia*, first matter, out of which things "cohere." In the 1855 Preface the attributes of the great poet "are called up of the float of the brain of the world . . ." In "I Sing the Body Electric" the end of the sixth section runs: "Do you think matter has cohered together from its diffuse float, and the soil is on the surface, and water runs and vegetation sprouts, / For you only, and not for him and her?" I quote another use in a context reminiscent of the "Ferry" poem and others I have quoted here:

I swear I think there is nothing but immortality!
That the exquisite scheme is for it, and the nebulous float
*   is for it, and the cohering is for it!*
And all preparation is for it—and identity is for it—and
*   life and materials are altogether for it!*
                    (*"To Think of Time," Lines 119–21*)

The use of the word in "Crossing Brooklyn Ferry" obviously refers to a procreative act, and this sense is approached in this line referring to wisdom in "Song of the Open Road":

Something there is in the float of the sight of things that
*   provokes it out of the soul.*
                    (*Line 82*)

Even a shift in meaning to "float" as a noun indicating a distance traversed retains the connection with generation:

I too have bubbled up, floated the measureless float, and
*   been washed on your shores . . .*
                (*"As I Ebb'd With the Ocean of Life," Line 42*)

The last two quotations of my train link up with the sense I attribute to the word in the "Ferry" poem, that is, generative fluid, semen:

If I, you, and the worlds, and all beneath or upon their
*   surfaces, were this moment reduced back to a*
*   pallid float, it would not avail in the long run.*
                    (*"Song of Myself," Section 45, Line 22*)

This is the press of a bashful hand, this the float and odor
*   of hair . . .*
                    (*"Song of Myself," Section 19, Line 7*)

(The last quotation suggests a displacement of "odor" from "float" to "hair.")

If we now return to the line which I have been boggling over,

I too had been struck from the float forever held in
solution,

(Section 5, Line 62)

it is clear that the rather extraordinary force of this line comes from a confluence of the resonance of light and semen: to be "struck" from the "float" is to be a chosen seed. The 1855–6 notebook originally had "cohered"; this was canceled for "was struck," and the 1856 edition substitutes "had been struck." We may now add that receiving "sustenance" from things, swallowing the "float," is parallel to being bathed in earthly light; we move in the psychic space in which Whitman's libidinized body is extended, and in which planetary motion is common to him and the sun, likewise libidinized.

Our clearest statement of the mythic core so far is from "The Song of the Answerer," "in him perceive themselves as amid light." But our agent is not simply the emitter of light and generative fluid; he is also, and reciprocally, passive to the earthly light and defined by it as a body, an identity who in the poem "Look'd at the fine centrifugal spokes of light round the shape of my head in the sunlit water."

Can we rationalize our conclusion into apprehensible shape? It is a highly plausible observation that the dreamer is both subject and object in his dream. The whole of the presented scene is, in a dream, the body. In the poem this is what the body becomes. The light and the float are that with which this extended body is correlative. We may now

quote with somewhat more assurance the line which refers
to the "dumb, beautiful ministers":

> *We use you and do not cast you aside—we plant you*
> *permanently within us . . .*

The paradox of democratic idealism has not been solved,
is, in fact, logically insoluble, but something of the character of the psychic space it seeks to create may be learned
from the Whitman of 1855 and 1856.

But what of the complex of centrality? Is this what it
means, to say that Whitman is both a body, a thing acted
upon, and an agent, the light which defines all bodies (or,
as I have extended it, defines all the objects of the presented scene)? Very nearly, but something more explicit
must be said about the overwhelming need that the complex seeks to supply. Whitman's poem was originally
called "Sun-Down Poem," yet the sun is twice in the final
version, three times in the first version, spoken of as "half
an hour high." This sun, both setting and rising, is wholly
characteristic of the complex of centrality which appears
to have at its root twin impulses: total submission to the
father, submission to sexual invasion, and a megalomanic
defense against that impulse, a power to emit sunlight, an
overwhelming power. Out of this situation arises the desperate assertion that one is poised or balanced in a "place,"
an attempt to bound a psychic space terrifyingly open, in
which things leave their place at the price of annihilation.[20]
(I need not point out that Whitman is breathing over our
shoulders here.) A quotation Róheim makes from a Japa-
nese chronicle may help to illustrate the character of
Whitman's emotional need:

In an official decree of the year 646 the Emperor of Japan is described as "the incarnate god who governs the universe." "In ancient times he was obliged to sit on the throne for some hours every morning with the imperial crown on his head but to sit altogether like a statue without stirring either hands or feet, head or eyes, nor indeed any part of his body because by this means it was thought he could preserve peace and tranquillity in his empire." [21]

To be everywhere, to be an all-powerful arranger of his world, this imperial self must sit just exactly there. In this case psychotic fantasy was public duty. But it may be objected that the notion of an imperial line breaches an important aspect of our myth: if the self is to extend out to the utter edge of things, it must be nobody's child, abolish time and surrender the prospect of any cumulation—the "dumb real objects" it possesses at this instant are to define eternity. Wallace Stevens's emperor is exemplary in this respect:

> *Call the roller of big cigars,*
> *The muscular one, and bid him whip*
> *In kitchen cups concupiscent curds.*
>
> .   .   .   .   .
>
> *Let be be finale of seem.*
> *The only emperor is the emperor of ice cream.*[22]

This enforces the point that what is indeed imperial resides in the moment, in a relation to the transient. There is an amusing and not insignificant foretaste of Stevens's poem in the third section of Whitman's:

The scallop-edged waves in the twilight, the ladled cups,
The frolicsome crests and glistening . . .

(Line 44)

The "ladled cups" offer themselves as "sustenance" for the soul; they are the ice cream of eternity. But of course this "roller of big cigars" is from the dialectic world of contrariety, of penis and vagina, rather than that of the all-engrossing self. Whitman's acknowledgment of that world of contrariety in the sixth section must be described.

As I have already suggested, the emotional weight of this section falls, rather unexpectedly, on the line

Saw many I loved in the street or ferry-boat or public
assembly, yet never told them a word . . .

(Line 81)

But its opening (in the 1881 version, lines 65–77) connects Whitman's own pains and difficulties with those of the social, heterosexual world in which people are bounded chiefly by one another rather than by the kind of myth that the complex of centrality gives rise to in the "Ferry" poem.

I quote these opening lines as they originally appeared in 1856:

It is not upon you alone the dark patches fall,
The dark threw its patches down upon me also,
The best I had done seemed to me blank and suspicious,
My great thoughts as I supposed them were they not in
reality meagre? Would not people laugh at me?
It is not you alone who know what it is to be evil,
I am he who knew what it was to be evil,
I too knitted the old knot of contrariety,
Blabbed, blushed, resented, lied, stole, grudged,
Had guile, anger, lust, hot wishes I dared not speak,

> *Was wayward, vain, greedy, shallow, sly, a solitary*
> *committer, a coward, a malignant person.*
> *The wolf, the snake, the hog, not wanting in me,*
> *The cheating look, the frivolous word, the adulterous*
> *wish, not wanting,*
> *Refusals, hates, postponements, meanness, laziness, none*
> *of these wanting . . .*

One of the things we notice first is that the light and flood motifs are here explicitly opposed by "dark patches" which "fall." The lounger at the rail who is at the same time the shaman will be translated, "though I stop here to-day and to-night," and there is a reference to a "flicker of black contrasted with wild red and yellow light" from the foundry chimneys. But this Manichaean opposition isn't developed; Whitman is far from Melville. Another and more central point is that the voice in the poem does not say that he includes all these intimate emotions of doubt and shame, and all the classical distortions of will that he lists. They are in the past for him. (What often happens in Whitman is that he catches up, say, the "gray-faced onanist" or the "venerealee.") Here the voice is viewing the world with the "free sense" which enables him to grasp it all without these distortions. (This was not so clear before 1871, when Whitman dropped a line from the ninth section, following the present seventh line, in which he repeated a part of his list of contrarieties.) One suggestive contrast between the two modes of consciousness in the poem emerges when we juxtapose the spokes of light diverging with mathematical precision from the image of the head in the water with the "knot of contrariety."

The poem as finally published by Whitman establishes

a sharp distinction between these two modes of consciousness: the one based on guilt, and the other based on the "free sense" of the ninth section—the same contrast I established above between being a "solitary committer" and the triumphantly guilt-free fusing and pouring of the eighth section.

We must grant the appropriateness of a comparison with Henry James: when Whitman, in this instance, sinks the poet in the poem, he becomes most completely the poet. The third section of the poem is unmatched in him or any one else in the nineteenth century as an American landscape rendered in words; the poem as a whole can be compared only with "Song of Myself." My description suggests an extraordinary extrapolation: in the poem in which the psychotic nucleus, the complex of centrality, is most elegantly presented, in which Whitman is at once fed by the world and feeds the world, subdued to the light and overmasters the light, he also manages to produce guilt-harried humanity, and the scene of the harbor and the cities struck with light. The whole shining, flowing world rises up within the mythical body, and is shown to waking men.

We have no problems with the passive term of the complex of centrality in this poem; a Whitman imaged in the water and describing himself as a negligent lounger is familiar. My explication includes, however, the active term as well, the shaman who confronts the sun "face to face." What is his relation to the poet? A full answer would require an essay as long as this chapter; a brief answer is simply that in this poem the poet is master. Were he not, I

should not have been able to produce the figure of the shaman.

The dimensions of the problem of talking sense about
Whitman show up with greater clarity in "Crossing
Brooklyn Ferry" than in any other poem. We must take
account of the shaman making his myth to act as a spell on
us, the characterization of the consciousness of interde-
pendent persons as guilt-ridden, the glories of the world of
appearance offered us—offered, we might say, as evidence
for the supremacy of the imperial consciousness—and,
finally, the poet himself, who finds a form in which the
seascape, the cities, the two consciousnesses, and the agent
of change may all appear. To name Whitman is to refer to
a phenomenon no less complex than this.

Chapter V

The Golden Bowl
as a Cultural Artifact

Henry James came to his modern celebrity as the hero of art, the man who had committed the novel to form as decisively as the fifteenth century had committed painting to perspective. In the 1940's and 1950's he had a peculiarly privileged position. Critics and writers were so entranced by his formal accomplishment that they were impatient with any reference to the fact that if his predecessors lacked his form, he lacked their stubborn, plural matter, especially in the later work. The penumbra of possibility which surrounded a thicket of social circumstance in the nineteenth-century novel vanished in James. His were works fully controlled, fully comprehended by their maker, and they dealt with matters that could be resolved in talk. There was a marked attenuation of the notion of human agency in them; what could be known, rather than what could be done, was the characteristic focus. Unlike the work of the modernists with whom James was often read, his works did not deal with cultural crises, with situations in which what had been thought to be the limits of the human condition were tested or passed. T. S. Eliot remarked that the hero of a James novel was a "social entity," contrived of course for the occasion.[1] (Its archetype is no doubt James's own family at breakfast.) In retrospect it may seem odd that readers of Joyce, Yeats, Rilke, Kafka, and Conrad tacitly put James in their company. These last had started from a different point in time, and from the perception that western culture was *in extremis;* in modernism writers with antecedents in the great romantic line face and encounter the breakdown of moral, social, and religious order, spelling out the consequences in poems or fictions. Briefly, God dies and Stephen Dedalus goes to work. James's part in all this is nil. His world, his experienced world, offers no extremities. His lack of imaginative preparation for those which actually touched him made him liable to panic. But his recovery from these episodes was marked by a reinstitution of his total imaginative order; he was quite incapable of learning anything from the modern world in which he lived his last years (anything, that is, which would lead him to revise his sense of what human powers there were and how they ought to be exercised). His cultural occasion was a quite different one. In him the nascent imperial self conquers the great world of European culture and art and carries it home in triumph. The venture was launched in the 1870's and is achieved with the publication of *The Golden Bowl.* This is his primary significance as a figure in cultural history. Europe was beautiful, bloody, greedy, sexually charged, publicly imperial. Its achieved forms had to be rescued for the uses of the undivided consciousness. The emotional starting point was that of Emerson and Whitman, but the accomplishment of the imaginative task called for a distinct and perhaps greater kind of genius: the undivided self must encompass a simulacrum of the varieties of experience and give them a totally coherent form.

There is no precise parallel in imaginative achievement for this conquest. There is a very nearly precise parallel with respect to the psychological and social consequences in the work of Norman O. Brown: he too reduces the stubborn oppositions of Freud's world and accomplishes the subjection of imperial power, acquisitiveness, and heterosexuality to the undivided consciousness. He completes his intellectual account by rescuing poetry from contemporary society in *Love's Body*, just as James had rescued achieved European forms in his fiction, *The Golden Bowl*. In fact, as we shall see, the two titles are ultimately much the same in meaning: form charged with post-heterosexual love. William Troy put it with final authority many years ago; the object of James's love is "the body of humanity stretched out in imagination in time and space." [2]

Those who read James in conjunction with the modernists were therefore not really mistaken. What they failed to see was that the vision of extremity provoked by the death of God was not James's, his imagined world was one in which the god was nascent, struggling to be born. James's relation to extremity was established by the nature of his consciousness of the world, not by what he saw in it. His was the world of a post-social consciousness to which these states had begun to pay imaginative homage long before Europe had fully envisaged it. *Emerson comes before Nietzsche* is the formula we must get through our heads. James's consciousness was primarily oral, as is the one that Brown celebrates. It could not comprehend and mourn or celebrate the lapsing of a social and religious order which it was not initially able to take in. It was not dialectical, not dramatic, not heterosexual, it contained nothing incommensurate with itself. Whatever it ingested could be rendered in talk.

One of the reasons that the strong chronological improbability of associating James with modernism went unregarded was that the first widespread flush of enthusiasm for his work in the 1940's was concomitant with the failure of our sense of literature as time-bound, as dependent on its cultural occasion. T. S. Eliot's insistence that the essential tradition in literary works *was* literary had a great deal to do with this, as did the failure of American Marxist criticism, the last gasp of explicit concern with the social meaning of art. Only fusty professors were concerned with "background," unless it took on the explicitly trans-cultural grandeur of myth and symbol, in which case it wasn't background any longer but a set of leitmotivs for the human condition in general. In these circumstances those who wrote about James had a luxurious romp within the circle of his own presumptions about his means and ends. There was a great deal to explore, and James's marvelous internal consistency made the rewards almost certain. R. P. Blackmur was one of the most gifted of these internal explorers, a fact which makes his final apostasy, in his second introduction to *The Golden Bowl*, a matter of great interest. F. W. Dupee's book on James, the best single book we have, is of course written from within by a critic whose sensibility is closely akin to James's own. Leon Edel's biography has a thousand Freudian peepholes, but no doorway which takes us outside James.[3] (The feebleness of such categories as the "psychological novel" or of the characterization of James as a sort of Balzac of the moral life seems obvious.)

The result of these cultural circumstances was that James was not recognized as an event in the history of the western imagination, the bearer of an exemplary neurosis, who may in this respect be compared to Augustine, Luther, Swift, and Rousseau. In 1947, when I first suggested this, I encountered a good deal of incomprehension. In the intervening years the context in which such assertions may be made has been more fully established by the confluent effect of a number of men: Eric Auerbach, Hans Jonas, E. R. Dodds, Norman Cohn, Erik Erikson, Eric Heller, Michael Walzer, Bruno Snell, all of whom, despite the variety of their disciplines and methodological emphases, have a common concern with the historical relationships of culture to works of the imagination and the psychic needs and commitments these express.

In *The American Henry James* I argued the virtual identity of what I called the "morality" of Henry James with that of his father, who had made a system of the self and the world as inclusive, as apocalyptic, and even more boring than that of Blake's prophetic books—with which it had important points of contact through Swedenborg. In this and the following chapter I wish to supply the necessary complements of that thesis: an account of James's own emotional commitments and of his relation to those other Americans who worked by incorporation, Emerson and Whitman. James is son to his father, to "father's ideas," to an American cultural strain, but most centrally, and in a mode which includes all these, he is son of his works. In them he learned to surrender agency, and a part of his autonomy as a person in order to take it all back in another form. *The Golden Bowl* is his most splendid feat of reduction in which the plural, acquisitive heterosexual world is caught in the net of his consciousness, and he permits the shining, flapping beasts to be seen before he immobilizes them forever. It is a work of great imaginative generosity and bravery, and yet it is terrible, as R. P. Blackmur finally saw. I will return to his last treatment of the book at the end of this chapter to show that the terror is not James's but Blackmur's, mine, perhaps yours.

Let us now examine *The Golden Bowl*, first with a more or less straight face, then with the wryness that the comprehension of a joke turned bitter enforces. It is hard to exaggerate the strangeness of this book for the wholly unprepared reader. The most suggestive literary comparison is that put forward by Francis Fergusson, who found it akin to the dramas of Racine.[4] Undoubtedly, some such process of reduction and abstraction has taken place. Motives stalk in robes of glory, yet there is no visualized scene, and no temptation to quote speeches. The man who set out to quote would find himself unable to put a stop; he would have to go on, and in the end he would deliver the whole book, display the whole tightly woven carpet—a tug on one corner pulls the whole thing. We cannot too often remind ourselves that it was spoken, dictated—as James put it to his amanuensis, Theodora Bosanquet, "pulled out of me" like yards of shining tissue. There is an amusing and significant account of Finley Peter Dunne's meeting with James at Edith Wharton's. Dunne reported to her that he had been dazzled, but had felt like saying, "Just pit it right up into Popper's hand" —one might fairly ache for the conclusive turn, but the voice went on.[5] James, as we are assured, didn't actually stammer; no doubt there were hesitations, moments in which the material was massing, yet no real prospect of full stop, of intermission. What was to be set forth had manifold connections and qualifications, but the language served, grammar never buckled under the strain, the verbs worked, the conjunctions subordinated, the marvelous tide flowed on, betraying its own pleasure in its sufficiency and fullness with adverbs which often seem to refer not so much to the wonders of the situation as to the marvel that is the total fact, the fact that it is all being said so well.

James's original notebook entry for *The Golden Bowl* has to do with a father and daughter, each of whom marries only to discover that their spouses are lovers. There are two volumes. In the first, called *The Prince*, it is the consciousness of Mrs. Assingham that presides; she is an imperfect Vergil to the man whose ancestor, Amerigo Vespucci, is said to have discovered America. In the second volume, Maggie Verver's consciousness frames the whole. The Prince, whose marriage Mrs. Assingham has brought about, is a consummate European, a product of centuries of breeding, whose family history commands a whole alcove of recorded splendors and crimes and follies in the

British Museum. His marriage to the American heiress Maggie Verver seems almost an affair of state, a final conjunction of the most exquisite qualities attributable to Europe and America. The innocence, good faith, and overwhelming financial power of the Ververs must, however, come to terms with their final acquisitions, the Prince and Charlotte, whom Mr. Verver marries. Two forms of consciousness must be reconciled with one another, and when they are the novel ends. The book imagines the realization of that "sublime consensus" between America and Europe which James had anticipated so many years before in writing his dialogue on George Eliot.[6] We should note that the world of the novel is claustral, that is, the intercourse of three couples—the Prince and Princess; Adam Verver and his wife, Charlotte; and Colonel and Mrs. Assingham —is rarely complicated, and then only incidentally, by the presence of other persons. This small and endlessly voluble cast has given some people the impression that the novel is an interminable process of scorekeeping in which each character reckons up the state of his or her feelings, attitudes, and expectations in relation to all the rest after every little shift of the balance of forces among them. Such readers have failed to be enchanted. But those who now profess an interest in James have tended increasingly to speak of *The Golden Bowl* as his greatest achievement.

The visible things James marshals are those necessitated by the idea, the reconciliation of the form of consciousness represented by the Prince and made explicit by Mrs. Assingham with that represented by Adam Verver and his daughter and made explicit at the end by Maggie herself. The scene of the novel is a strictly occasional London. The Paris of Proust and the Dublin of Joyce are first of all accepted, taken for granted; they are the ground on which and against which the writers work. But the London of *The Golden Bowl* is a scene constituted in order that certain things may appear, just as Dante's Inferno is constituted in order that certain qualities of the Florentines may be made manifest. Consciousness is not the interior world of the novel: there is no interior world, and no persons whose inner struggle is the result of outward circumstance. There is no such division as that between the inward and the outward at all. Appearance is wholly in the service of consciousness, and nothing appears which is not in the full Blakean sense the product of consciousness. There is nothing intractable, unknowable, unshaped to human ends. When the reconciliation of which I spoke has been effected, no difficulties will remain, no questions will be unanswered. There will be no occasion, as in Victorian novels, to wish the characters Godspeed, for no scene on which they may be imagined to persist will remain. Once consciousness is one, the possibilities of change need no longer concern us. That James should finally have written a novel in which the two loves (the first seeking to possess, the second to celebrate the world) were the subject,[7] and titled it *The Golden Bowl*, a title of which the biblical meaning is of course "mind" or consciousness, makes a very elegant intellectual conclusion to his career. The subject is now the nature of the way in which the world is grasped. It is true that this had been of very great importance in other works (as it is in *The Portrait of a Lady*), but in all the precedent works there is some sop of worldly interest at which the reader may snap, some concession to the idea that there are many stories of which this is one, with its particular fillip of difference. Here it is the story of all stories that James is telling, the myth of consciousness itself.

There is a more generalized sop of an apparent sort: this is the idea of the novel itself, of the novel as a literary form, which is the appearance *The Golden Bowl* presents and finally snatches away, leaving us alone with the gods sitting alone. Such a work utterly annihilates the circumstantiality and time-bound character of the tradition from which it—oh so deliberately!—purports to come and may be seen in the generic terms of allegory, or cosmic myth. It was so, that in the light of the system of the elder James, I saw *The Golden Bowl* in *The American Henry James*. It cast a mythological reflection of a vast and cloudy sort, and I tried to read it as faithfully as I could. But in that book I was not ready to develop the notion of the hypertrophied or imperial self (although I advanced it), nor was I quite so clearly aware of the relevance of the terms of psychic need and commitment which James's work entails.

We cannot, it turns out, do even approximate justice to *The Golden Bowl* without referring to the ways in which the overweening demands of the incarnate child, and the reflection of these in the suprahuman images of myth and the severe abstractions of metaphysics, find a place in it, and range below and above the expectations of the conversable novel-reading world. Not willing to acknowledge the emotional returns they were getting from the book— the assurance of the self's dominion over the world, assured in fact by their theory of art that to acknowledge these returns was to be deprived of art itself (as if by some magical transgression like stepping on a line in the pavement)—the critics have treated the Prince and Charlotte, for example, as if they were characters in a nineteenth-century novel, and asked why Charlotte's magnificence must be effectually denied, and the splendid Prince subdued to Maggie. To this question one must reply that that is what you must do if you wish to possess the whole world: eradicate its most stubborn pluralism, which is represented by the physical and emotional difference between men and women. To understand this would have precluded the pleasure they sought, and so it remained an open secret. Another question, even more serious, because closer to the secret demand that they be given possession of the world of those who bound themselves to art, is "How can Adam be guiltless?" (He has the wrong possession—money.) I will come to that question in my promised section of wryness. Meanwhile, I should like to set forth what happens in the book a little more fully.

The representation of the two loves in the novel runs through the whole fabric, but its emblems are the two golden bowls, the cracked bowl of historic human consciousness lived in time and space and the bowl to which Maggie refers, "the bowl as it was to have been." The first bowl, made by a "lost art"—that of the creator —in a "lost time"—the beginning of things—is the emblem of Eve, who incited us to eat, who launched us on the course of acquisitiveness we have ever followed. It is likewise the emblem of Charlotte Stant. The second bowl is the emblem of the Prince as Maggie finally enjoys him, the bowl to which Adam Verver compares him. It is one of

James's cosmic jokes to make the Prince resentful that he and Charlotte are being treated like Adam and Eve, a resentment which can be assuaged in only one way, by enacting the fall in its Babylonian version, and lying together. The cracked bowl or Bloomsbury cup whose discovery ties the Prince and Charlotte together in Maggie's mind is a wider emblem still. It stands for human life lived under the dominion of caste, of acquisitiveness, of sexuality, of the practical and political intelligence ("What," asks Fanny Assingham, "is morality but high intelligence?" [8]), and the Prince may be said to add science to the list in reflecting on the fabulous activities of Adam Verver ("What was science but the absence of prejudice backed by the presence of money?" [9]).

Many things go to smash with the bowl, but of course the most striking casualty is sexuality. The Prince fills his Charlotte but once. Thereafter, "the twentieth woman," as he calls her, can serve him no more; he can't any longer get his identity at that shop, the rule of the lordly male is over. He is, with all the rest of existence, subject to Maggie, consciousness undivided. I have described the stages of this cosmic comedy more fully elsewhere: [10] Charlotte and the Prince are driven into each other's arms, only to be separated forever. "What else can we do, What in all the world else?" is the cry with which Charlotte precipitates the adultery, [11] and it is plain that in the world, the worldly world, there is nothing else left. The realm of appearance has been bought up by Adam in its final form of works of art. These voices of silence are endlessly to hymn redeemed humanity in the museum in American City. The translation of the Prince and Charlotte is the last and most difficult of the imaginative chores of consciousness. But I am ahead of the story.

The bowl is smashed by Fanny Assingham, whom Maggie has called on to interpret the significance of its testimony to the intimacy of the Prince and Charlotte. Fanny's excremental name, and the office of the great whore she here performs, holding up "a golden cup in her hand full of abomination and filthiness of her fornication," are sufficient reminders of the nature of the love she sponsors and the intelligence she employs. Fighting in behalf of appearance itself, here figured as the apparent propriety of the two marriages she has made, she breaks the bowl because it is evidence that the marriages are lies, false forms. But she gives the show away while trying to preserve it: the Prince enters and is confronted by what he has done; denial becomes assertion. With all appearance gone, the Prince turns helplessly to Maggie.

James's second great stroke of irony is the fashion in which Maggie carries out a redeemer's office. She enters into the game of keeping up appearances herself, that is, assumes "humanity," because she means to save the whole situation without telling the lovers or her father anything about it. She goes into society, becomes fully subject to the world's love of what shows, by battling in secrecy for her father and her husband.

In a brilliant scene at Fawns, the temporary resting place of Adam's rarest acquisitions, Maggie paces the terrace, glancing as she does so at the adulterers, who are seated at cards with her father, and Mrs. Assingham within the house. She has had an impulse to behave like a wronged wife and an outraged daughter; as she passes the great, empty, brightly lit drawing room, she imagines it as "a scene she might people either with serenities and dignities and decencies, or with terrors and shames and ruins, things as ugly as those formless fragments of her golden bowl she was trying so hard to pick up." But James's Maggie is totally incapable of an action which takes the risks of impulse and passion, or a scene in which inner pressures mold outer events. She here figures the turbulence of passion as so remote as to be exotic, a "wild eastern caravan" which disappears before it reaches her. This refusal to be what she humanly and dramatically is, a woman whose sense of her self as wife and daughter has been violated, marks her determination to be what Whitman's agent is in "Crossing Brooklyn Ferry," the apostle of a unitary consciousness. Her glimpse of the "provocation of opportunity which had assaulted her, within, on her sofa, as a beast might have leaped at her throat," is a revealing figurative inversion. Had she so acted to denounce the guilty, she would have been overcome—this is what the figure announces. In other words, action fractures the unitary consciousness. A total order or nothing is what she actually demands. The sixth section of Whitman's poem is a close functional analogue; we even have the use of theatrical terms to describe the rejected forms of consciousness in both instances.

But James has a story to tell. He solves the problem of Maggie's assumption of humanity with extraordinary virtuosity. The sign that she is in the world of action, but not of it, is her response to Charlotte's challenge as to whether there is anything that the Princess has to complain of.

Maggie's denial is her redeemer's passion. But the fascinating fact is that if we try to imagine what the meaning of refusing to tell this lie would have been, we realize that it would have destroyed not only the marriages, but the basis of Maggie's character, the attempt to realize the "bowl as it was to have been."

Maggie's reward is the isolation and exile of Charlotte, who is told nothing by the Prince, nothing by Maggie, nothing by her contemplative husband, Adam, whom Maggie sees as "weaving his spell" and holding the marvelous feral creature in leash. Appearance is now completely at the service of reality. James's method in writing the book has become an event in the book itself. The "bowl as it was to have been" comes into being in the person of the Prince full of Maggie's love—an inversion of the earlier bowl: Charlotte full of the Prince.

This abridged account of the struggle which fuses the two forms of consciousness, America and Europe, appearance and reality, has neglected Adam Verver. In him James puts before us a familiar antithesis within the nineteenth-century American: his restlessly striving, continent-embracing, acquisitive self is combined in Adam with the impulse to range the greatest of human accomplishments before his fellows in the greatest of museums. But the cliché is transcended when James insists on Adam's impeccable taste. This man whose brain has been "a strange workshop of fortune" had come in a night to realize

the affinity of Genius, or at least of Taste, with something in himself—with the dormant intelligence of which he had thus almost violently become aware and that affected him as changing by a mere revolution of the screw his whole intellectual plane. He was equal somehow with the great seers, the invokers and encouragers of beauty—and he didn't after all perhaps dangle so far below the great producers and creators. He had been nothing of that kind before—too decidedly, too dreadfully not; but now he saw *why* he had been what he had, why he had failed and fallen short even in huge success; now he read into his career, in one single magnificent night, the immense meaning it had waited for.[12]

Nothing has shocked James's most devoted readers more profoundly than this. A millionaire become a "seer," in the Emersonian prophetic strain, who envisions and acts to bring about an esthetic consummation for the vast continent. This must be a lapse of taste and conception on the part of the writer! As readers of a cultural document, we have no such *parti pris;* for the moment let the fact and the apparent anomaly stand for themselves. We may simply note that in Adam Verver the two forms of consciousness have been reconciled before the novel begins; their reconciliation in him is a datum of the story. He had had, as James puts it, "to *like* forging and sweating" in order to become what he now is. His greedy self acted to an end of which it was not aware to give the self that seeks "communications and contacts" for the objects of its love a total fulfillment. Acquisition was a necessary prelude to celebration. Money may be taken for a finality, as it is by Abel Gaw in *The Ivory Tower.* But apparently it need not be. Everything depends on the use you make of it. There are two loves, two ways of taking the world. *What is taken is the same thing*. It is simply put to different uses, as the shellwork of legend about Shakespeare is captured by the curator for the uses of art in *The Birthplace*. For the tourists it had been a kind of psychic money to feed their self-importance, money of which the definition is that anything in which form is made subservient to matter is crap, is, if you wish to use that vocabulary, evil.

The same thing may be said of language itself. Everything depends on the use you make of it. In James's famous passage on the nightmare of which the Galerie d'Apollon at the Louvre was the scene, he encounters and repels that aspect of himself which would take possession of the world in the acquisitive mode.[13] His mode is of course the mode of celebration, that of the writer, the use of human speech. A part of James's praise of speech in one of the lectures he delivered in the United States in 1905, just after the publication of *The Golden Bowl*, will help us to understand his sense of how speech could be used and misused. The title of the lecture is "The Question of Our Speech."

All life therefore comes back to the question of our speech, the medium through which we communicate with each other; for all life comes back to the question of our relations with each other. These relations are made possible, are registered, are verily constituted by our speech, and are successful (to repeat my word) in proportion as our speech is worthy of its great human and social function; is developed, delicate, flexible, rich—an adequate accomplished fact. The more it suggests and expresses the more we live by it—the more it promotes and enhances life. Its quality, its authenticity, its security, are hence supremely important for the general multifold opportunity, for the dignity and integrity, of our existence.

James of course envisions speech as the primary means of communion with his fellows. The consummations, the unions, we achieve with our bodies meant little to him. As he says later on in his address, speech has importance "as the very hinge of the relations of man to man." Yet the speech of American youngsters is often "a mere helpless slobber of vowel sounds." American speech is further endangered by immigrants who, linguistically speaking, "dump their mountains of promiscuous material into the foundations of the American." Earlier he had characterized the unconcern of Americans with the question of their speech: its processes are referred to as "matters going on . . . in the dark," and, he continues, "to eat in the dark . . . is to run the chance . . . of besmearing our persons." [14]

The violence of the disgust for bad speech which he exhibits here has to do with the fact that for him speech is a deeply sexualized activity, and we catch a clear intimation in his phrasing that bad speech has an excrementitious character. It is perhaps hardly news that James's emotional life centered about his mouth and anus, but it has surely not been discussed enough by those who are concerned with his absorption in the matter of literary form. The emotional ambience of a mouth-centered consciousness is after all distinct from that of a genitally centered consciousness. The impulse of the former in this case is to reduce the latter imaginatively to a kind of greed, a "famished appetite," as the elder James phrases it. This impulse is enacted in *The Golden Bowl*. What Norman O. Brown and the existentialist theologian Berdyaev advocate, what Swedenborg and Blake and the elder Henry James had earlier envisioned, an androgynous divine man, can come into being only if the genitally centered consciousness is banished. This is what happens at the end of *The Golden Bowl*.

The myth of consciousness, the story of all stories, must have a subject as well as an object. Maggie is that subject and Maggie-cum-Prince is the divine man. From the point of view of poor, sexually sundered humanity, Maggie's final words about Charlotte sound profoundly cruel. She says to the Prince toward the end:

> "She's wonderful and beautiful, and I feel somehow as if she were dying. Not really, not physically," Maggie went on—"she's naturally, splendid as she is, far from having done with life. But dying for us—for you and me; and making us feel it by the very fact of there being so much of her left. Only, as you also say, for others."
>
> The Prince smoked hard a minute. "As you say, she's splendid, but there is—there always will be—much of her left. Only, as you also say, for others."
>
> "And yet I think," the Princess returned, "that it isn't as if we had wholly done with her. How can we not always think of her? It's as if we had needed her, at her own cost, to build us up and start us." [15]

Adam's money had been magically transformed into the voices of consciousness, the works of art. Now Charlotte, whom the Prince had seen as a long loose silk purse full of money, has been spent. The Eve was needed to show us what we had been doing in trying to make selves through acquisition rather than through celebration. (The notion of evil as a finality is quite as far from James's imagination as it is from Blake's.) Charlotte is subdued to her final use as cicerone of a museum. A museum is where you don't own anything. The motive force which had driven us through history is no longer required. Once the Prince had been shown what he was up to, in the scene in which he confronts the meaning of the broken bowl, there is what I have called "a cosmic change of guard." Maggie sees "that her husband would have . . . a new need of her . . ." [16] and a little later develops the idea further:

> It had operated on her now to the last intensity, her glimpse of the precious truth that by her helping him, helping him to help himself, as it were, she should help him to help *her*. Hadn't she fairly got into his labyrinth with him?—wasn't she indeed in the very act of placing herself there, for him, at its centre and core, whence on that definite orientation and by an instinct all her own, she might securely guide him out of it? [17]

She is more than guide now, she is all he sees, or, we can turn it about, all they will ever see is what she sees in him. What he sees in her is simply a mode of seeing, the final one. Hence he repeats what she says in the paragraphs just quoted. They are eager for a final consummation, so eager indeed that James can figure it as having a tragic finality. The Prince returns to the room after the departure of Adam and Charlotte Verver. He has confided the hapless Principino, whose parents are about to blend, to Miss Bogle. As he enters, Maggie takes it in that she is to be "paid in full." Charlotte, the splendid Charlotte, she has been assured (in a mute colloquy with her father) is not to be wasted. When Amerigo enters she renews her assertion of Charlotte's splendor, as if for a last certification from the Prince, that he is content with the use to which Charlotte is to be put. Her splendor is "our help, you see," says Maggie. The Prince wants "too clearly" to please her. But his wish can never meet her on the plane of reasons. The drops spread evenly over his golden surface, to use Adam's figure about him, but never penetrate.[18] This second Adam must leave the thinking to the feminine principle or "conscience," as the elder James has it. But James leaves us in no doubt that he is hers forever, will hereafter see as she sees.

> " 'See'? I see nothing but *you*." And the truth of it had, with this force, after a moment, so strangely lighted his eyes that as for pity and dread of them, she buried her own in his breast." [19]

The shimmering, glancing character of *The Golden Bowl* for its reader, the impression that reading it is like playing a game in which we are always shuffling the same elements—once more we will explore the possibility of saying this or that with respect to its effect on, or meaning for, each of the four central characters—the conclusion of each episode usually takes the form of a definitive pronouncement that we can't *do* that (and "do" always means *say*) to Adam Verver, Father *and* cuckold. But this is just the sort of thing the reader might mutter to himself, there really isn't any such game, since there is no detached moment when the characters actually are, as Maggie says to Adam, "lying like gods together" and contemplating the intricate *contredanse* which is their total interrelatedness. The novel is always about its business, although it may sometimes seem to be a vast vegetable, an enormous exfoliation fertilized by a central core of nastiness, the insertion of that penis in that vagina.

But to put it this way is to err. I have used the transitive terms which denote heterosexuality, as if the loathed encounter itself had entered into, been apprehended imaginatively by James. But sexuality did not have a dialectic character for him. The reader may be tempted to bring forward the phallic assertiveness of the pagoda in Maggie's garden, which figures her dawning awareness of trouble in her life. But the pagoda's tallness and its exotic character are, curiously enough, Charlotte's. The Prince, we might remind ourselves, is always a bowl or a palace, something that contains. With the exception of a scene in which the Prince tries to seduce his newly suspicious wife, the primary form of sexuality in this myth of consciousness is connected with figures of consumption, and of money as both agent and object of consumption. Charlotte full of the Prince is the most direct meaning of the cracked bowl, but this is the consequence of their intimacy. The consummation itself is figured by the guilty pair at Matcham as their day together, "a great golden cup" which they will drain jointly.[20]

A group of figurative expressions for the emotional returns James's characters are after will show how completely consummation is identified with something taken in, like food, or stored away, like a precious possession. Figures which suggest an abandonment of one's self that results in a heightened sense of one's self and of the lover are absent. In *The Wings of the Dove* Densher forces Kate to sleep with him in his rooms in Venice by threatening to give up their scheme to inherit Milly's wealth. What he recalls about the experience is a "treasure" of memory. The Prince sees Charlotte at the opening of *The Golden Bowl* as a long, loose purse containing coins. What Strether of *The Ambassadors* sees in Chad's personal presence is that he has been enhanced, spiritually fattened, by his love affair. The mournful unfed consciousness of *The Sacred Fount* prowls about trying to find out who is feeding whom sexually, and the evidence that this feeding is going on is in the enhanced personal presences he meets. About Chad's gain in *The Ambassadors* there is the implication of thievery, and a brutal disregard of the fostering Mme. de Vionnet. The phrase I have quoted from the elder James is definitive. His spiritual socialism will lead to a world in which "famished appetite and mercenary lust" no longer exist. Perhaps Philip Roth's Portnoy has made it easier for us to see how the novelist imagined these things; "eating pussy" is perhaps as close as he can come to the unimaginable parental congress; it is like taking something into the mouth.

Since there is an emotional focus about questions of ingestion and excretion, we must expect deep ambivalences as well. What is prized and what is loathed are intimately involved with one another. The golden bowl is full of the filthiness of fornication. And that which is filthy about money is connected with sex. Densher's "treasure" is unclean not simply because he has bargained with Kate for the use of her body, but because sexuality itself is unclean. I have already mentioned Nanda Brookenham's comparison of herself to a pipe through which filth has passed, and we know that the filth consists in sexual chatter. When she speaks of it as sticking to her, we are led to think of feces.

Charlotte and the Prince, draining their cup, are feeding on the unclean. Charlotte, as I have noted, is seen by the Prince as a purse full of coins. Earlier, lounging before Bond Street windows, he had been confronted by shapes whose value was attested by the material of which they were made, just as in *The Wings of the Dove* the stuffed and corded shapes in the drawing-room of Britannia of the Market-Place, Mrs. Lowder, assert their value through their material fatness. These instances suffice to suggest that the filth of sexuality is intimately bound up with the question of stuff, material, and money. Money is most inclusively a profound inversion: it is that in which the form serves the material. It is of course deeply antipathetic to James that the value of anything should depend on quantity instead of form.

But this is secondary to James's root apprehension of

the matter, which is that of Freud, and of those who have pursued the Freudian insight, among them Marcuse and Norman O. Brown, that money and feces are imaginatively indissoluble. What is valued simply as material is assimilable to feces, to crap. To see Charlotte in the Prince's sexually acquisitive fashion—that of the lordly male—is to see her as full of money. Here James's imagination has first reduced heterosexual desire to a desire for what Melanie Klein calls "good body contents," what the infant initially desires of the mother, and then gone on to see those contents as the formed crap which is money.

This is consistently extended in James's work to an imaginative association with those whose "form" is but an attestation of material possessions, or of status externally conferred. Hence Lord "Mark" of *The Wings of the Dove* is named to suggest that he is simply that, a measured value. Strether, early in *The Ambassadors*, looks about him at the play and realizes that those he sees in the audience are externally defined as values; they are like coins.

We might be tempted to stop here with a rephrasing of the biblical apopthegm that the love of money, which is but a representation of the unformed, is the root of all evil. But this would suggest that James was a dualist, that he saw the world as divided between bad or unformed stuff and good or formed stuff. We can put his conviction with precision without making this split. To take the unformed for a finality is the root of all evil. If we extend this to money, that form designated to represent the unformed, and to all similarly external assertions of value, such as rank or a big balance at the banker's, we are in a position to see that James's world is not split, nor is he ever implicated in the notion that evil is absolute, and this for the very same reason that he will not grant even momentary fixity to the roles we play in life, including our sexual roles. (That such a man should have entertained the illusion that he could be a dramatist and gotten others to entertain it is an interesting fact about the conception of the drama in his time.)

We conclude, then, by admitting that the material the world offers is of but one sort, the stuff of experience is of but one sort, and that the only question is the question of how it is used, how it is taken; whether you seek to possess it or to use it to make those forms that celebrate life.[21] Henry James, I should say, analyzed himself completely, not in the sense that he concluded that he had one sort of emotional disposition as contrasted with another, but in the sense that he is in possession of a thoroughgoing account of his own emotional economy and emotional structure, which he extrapolates to cover the behavior of all the world; everybody takes things in either the right way or the wrong, although the fun lies in the question of all the possible shadings between the two. As to the heterosexual, it isn't a separate category at all, as I implied when discussing the Prince's figure for Charlotte; the heterosexual is simply an especially stubborn form of the selfish or acquisitive.

Our difficulty at this point lies in the very measure of James's success in making the things he made. They are so exquisitely distinct and complete that my exposition of their imaginative propinquity to the unclean, to, for example, the "mere helpless slobber of vowel sounds," the excrementitious expression James uses to characterize American speech, is hard to take in. But this is the very point. The line is so very fine between form and anality that it must be drawn with exquisite precision. Although geographic figures are inadequate, we may say that James's is not a world of the self and the other; it is a world more or less successfully incorporated in the web of related forms which is the product of consciousness; what is not incorporated is mere stuff, matter, the content of a newspaper—ultimately, crap.

But this, one might reply, is an extreme. James paid—did he not?—a very full tribute to the world of ostensible roles, to the world of the self and the other. Yes, he did, and I characterize that tribute more fully in the next chapter, but in the meantime our business is with *The Golden Bowl*, in which he dramatized the dispensability of that world of the self and the other, or, rather, the necessity of making it subordinate to the world of the undivided consciousness.

To come back to the *Bowl*—the novel is always about its business, pressing toward its imaginative end, and one of the things that needs most emphasis in this account is that that end is not some hidden one which James's unconscious pursues in spite of his overt intention: it is what James did, the end is right there, and we have brought a total conditioning and all the energy of denial to our reading. In the flush of our greatest enthusiasm, we must have wanted the emotional returns more than we wanted to acknowledge the conditions under which the novel yielded them. The novel pursues its emotional and intellectual goals quite openly.

If Maggie's possession of her Prince is taken for what it is, James's possession of his world, the book seems to me a wholly transparent and wholly successful rendering of what James sought to render. It is the myth of consciousness realized. Maggie may properly say with Adam, *"Le compte y est."* [22] It is indeed. And associating James with Maggie suggests something else. His own father had never gone near the Syracuse properties which provided his income. He had hardly liked "forging and sweating," as Adam Verver had. His acquisitive period had been spent in making theological notions and, as he tells us in his fragment of autobiography, growing spiritually fatter on self-righteous pride. But these are simply modes of acquisition. Priding yourself on your money or on your theological inventions comes down to the same thing. And what American "seer" had indeed put the Eve in leash, as Adam does Charlotte, and foreseen a triumphant imaginative issue for America itself? Whose life had indeed been like "the programme of a charity performance," as Maggie describes Adam's? The "great and deep and high little man" whom Maggie praises has more than a touch of James's own filial piety. The part the elder James plays in *The Tragic Muse* is minor compared to this one. [23] That "turn of the inward wheel," [24] which James sees as his father's sense of how all the appearances will be transformed into the forms which celebrate the divine-natural-humanity, is a figure precisely and appropriately associated with Adam's glimpse in a night of the fashion in which a "mere revolution of the screw" will enable him to "rifle the golden isles," [25] to come into guiltless possession on behalf of all America of the achieved forms of consciousness.[26] Part of the project of incorporating the world is incorporating father.

James's imagination lives hand to mouth, must forever ingest and render, must forever convert, must forever dabble in the filth that is the unformed in order to make the formed thing. We utterly fail to comprehend the necessities of the undivided self when we indignantly reject the possibility that Adam Verver can convert the crap which is his wealth into the guiltless possession of the forms that fill his museum, or that Maggie can convert the very fact of the adultery itself, the filthiest thing of all, into the most exquisite possession of all, the final luster of her Prince, stretched out in time and space, wholly suffused by her love, "the bowl as it was to have been." To take possession of the world as form is to take possession of the whole of the Prince, in whom the bloody, contradictory, wasteful past is summed up. Charlotte, we remember, is "the twentieth woman." Centuries of empire and ostensible male dominion, and the Eve all the while incessantly driving us to eat, all finally forced to say to Maggie, " 'See,' I see only you." Of course, James was quite sane enough to know that his playful apocalypse was a myth.

R. P. Blackmur, the critic who finally established James's tie with modernism for his generation, wrote two introductions to *The Golden Bowl*. Each is what the new criticism, perhaps following I. A. Richards, called a "reading." The use of the term suggested a full imaginative appropriation, starting up afresh with a work of importance, which characteristically was not thought of as demanding any reference to an existing set of critical observations, or even any principled stance on the part of an identifiable sensibility. The reading was felt to be congruent with a world in which works and criticism were, so to speak, coeternal—this meant that youngsters who undertook such criticism were supposed to leap into the game fully armed—a world in which the claims of tradition might be made only when the reader was assured that the announced conjunctions were themselves being made afresh. About the idea of the reading there is something akin to the imperialism which it was often designed to celebrate. A pure reading is probably a practical impossibility, but the tendency, the impulse toward a "total criticism," having your cake as you baked it, making the work while you read it, was widespread.

This impulse often puts Blackmur where no critic ought to be, between the writer's pen and his page, or at least acting as a passionate acolyte at the altar, watching the consummation of the sacred mystery. He was an extraordinary reader, one of those of whom students report that the work's coming into being was somehow enacted before their eyes. He attributes extraordinary awarenesses to his artists; his excuse is that they have been provoked in him. Both Henry Adams and Henry James are overborne by the variety and intensity of the responses to the creative situation Blackmur imputes to them. Part of the trouble is that Blackmur seems sure that they had his climate of awareness; historically speaking, this is simple nonsense.

They may have been more aware, or less, but they could hardly have been so exquisitely *au courant* with Blackmur as he believes.

Blackmur's two introductions to *The Golden Bowl* were published a decade or more apart. In the first, the forms of art seem to be breaking through to define the character of existence, and the primary word is "poetry":

> The imaginative mind must use many modes of seeing in order to come upon a single view and especially so when, as in our age, there is no existing single view to which the imagination gives universal credit and what is universal seems rather what is made fresh.[27]

One is momentarily startled to realize that the last clause is a compressed version of our original quotation from Emerson, "It seems to be true that the more exclusively idiosyncratic a man is, the more general and infinite he is, which, though it may not be a very intelligible expression, means, I hope, something intelligible." [28] But there is of course a signal difference: an essentially religious hope has been confided to the forms of art which are not in the least expected to create a grand recognition scene for humanity. Rather, our sense of our humanity is being entrusted to art, to something "made," quite as if art could always be counted on to enhance it. The leading motif of the first Preface to *The Golden Bowl* is that stated in the paragraph of quotation which follows (which suggests Santayana on the natural status of ideals in human life):

When set upon by the evil in life it is the good, in James, that in the instance perishes however it may endure in essence or ideal, in the heaven of man's mind. Here I think is the element in James' novels that gives them their fabulous air; we believe in them only as we believe in hellish or heavenly fables, as we might believe in some fabulous form of the uncreated shades of ourselves. These shades have always been the springs of poetry, of individual insight into collective moral experience and created images of moral beauty alike. They trouble our conscience and indeed are our conscience, not of particular ill doings or omission but of life itself; and so likewise these troublings teach us ways of love—of human relatedness —to which even as we see them we are inadequate but to which ever afterwards we aspire.[29]

In this Preface James's last three novels in order of composition, *The Ambassadors*, *The Wings of the Dove*, and *The Golden Bowl*, are accorded the status of a modern Divine Comedy, an extraordinary demonstration of what the thing "made fresh" can do for our sense of our humanity. Strether, Milly Theale, and Maggie Verver, the central figures of the last three novels, are themselves such exigent shades, "they suffer as shades always must in the anguish of the actual world, the certainty either of degradation or extinction, or both." They suffer in an ascending scale, which Blackmur compares to that of Dante. Strether suffers "all that is possible to the senses," Milly "what is possible as allegory or created meaning," and Maggie as does Beatrice from "the pangs of the highest human love." [30] In treating *The Golden Bowl* itself Blackmur is emphatic about the cost in life of Maggie's "moral beauty, or her conscience, or her new mode of love," which Charlotte is said to "repudiate," and Adam, sensibly, to flee. In this introduction the terms in which Blackmur examines the poetry of the new mode of love, in which Maggie and the Prince have both become "shades"—he says of their final embrace, "It was a shade embracing a shade, but in the shades of poetry" [31]—there is no intimation that James's art has anywhere betrayed life, but only that Maggie's good conscience has. There is no suggestion that one might question the authority of "shades" that are the "springs of poetry."

In the second introduction there is a total change of emphasis. It is now James himself who is charged with inhumanity growing out of a deep-seated impulse which the characters enact. Blackmur has returned upon himself in a striking way. He is apparently no longer willing to confide humanity to James's art. Blackmur was himself so influential and representative a figure in the movement to do just that that this turn is a rather important cultural symptom. I quote the most charged of his passages of protest, noting that his late-blooming humanism has put muscle on his prose.

It is the scene on the terrace that converts both the symbolic actions of the bowl and the image of the pagoda and the actions of love and marriage into actions of the Psyche, that human Psyche who, as Santayana somewhere puts it, after having surrendered everything insists that she has lost nothing. It is one of those lies by which we extend ourselves beyond humanity and degrade the humanity of others.

The instinct for this sort of action in James must have originated in some layer of the psyche much deeper than the imagination. Some might ally it with the instinct for death as in Freud's psychology or the ideal of Nirvana as in Buddhism, but these would only obliterate the action. In James the instinct attaches itself to life as directly as a leech or a tick to your arm; it means to do something with life—even with the life that has slipped or been taken away—that will in the end seem to the actor triumphant and an act of love.[32]

Blackmur cannot, it appears, bring himself to say, "That will seem to *James* triumphant and an act of love." But he has been horrified by what he has finally seen. There were of course two possibilities: first, James's view of humanity was such that *The Golden Bowl* did not appear profoundly cruel and wasteful to him; second, that he could not have failed of the full diapason of sympathy with humanity—he must at once have truly known and been truly in love with the horror he had invoked. In other words, Blackmur had lived inside James so long that he could not come out without leaving another kind of "shade" in the corpus, a Blackmur who had carried *The Four Quartets* inside with him, and was therefore sure that James was writing about

> *The greater torment*
> *Of love satisfied.*

But James's view of humanity was such that *The Golden Bowl* did not appear profoundly cruel and wasteful to him at all. The writer whom Blackmur had initially associated with Dante's inclusive vision of the human condition has become in his eyes a writer whose work degrades the humanity of others, one whose psyche shows a profound distortion. (The view of the first Preface appears to be the consequence of allowing himself to be so overwhelmed by his vision of the shaping power of imagination that he failed to preserve a conception not only of our humanity, but even of his own.) So the horror *The Golden Bowl* inspires is Blackmur's, is mine, is perhaps yours, but if we wish to imagine the undivided self, we had better face up to it: it is not felt by James.

Since his biographers have managed to get it into our heads, we have been clear that Whitman conceived of humanity rather differently: his sense of us as men and women and children is admitted to be distinct from that held in his time. The upshot is that we are not at war with Whitman's sense of the world. In fact we are able to grant it rather too easily, as I have pointed out. But in the case illustrated by Blackmur's shift of view, we have been hamstrung by a stubborn denial that James conceived men and women differently. We have gone right on treating the works as if they were not affected by a shift in the novelist's view of the matter to be treated. The religion of art had no such term as "inhumane" in its vocabulary. There was no way of editing the iconography of the imagination. In its realm whatever came into being had an equal right to come into being with every other thing. Whatever existed was right.

Chapter VI

Coming Out of Culture

The title of this chapter points to an event literally unrealizable before the last days. We still lead associated lives. It is to attempts to imagine such a consummation that I have devoted my chapters on Emerson and Whitman. Henry James's late work incarnates the claims of the imperial self in form—the esthetic shape of particular novels—and marks a further step in the process of our dissociation from the imaginative priority of communal life. As I have pointed out, the readiness of readers and critics to accept first James and then Whitman on their own radical terms had a cultural ground. We had somehow been prepared to grant a greater fullness of being to works of art than to our circumstanced lives. It was a provisional readiness, a momentary affair, like attending an Emerson lecture. But it happened.

I suggested in 1950 that our readiness to allow James to make a world for us might have arisen out of an overweening appetite for an articulation of moral order with experience—an appetite which had been defeated and derided by recent history.[1] Whatever the complex of reasons, we were receptive in the 1950's to Whitman's extortionate demand that the world be shaped as if he were its creator and mother, just as we had bowed to James's sense that the world had no compelling character and that he could rule it absolutely if he appeared to surrender everything to the form. The emotional returns were like those offered by Emerson (to whom we might logically have also responded in this period, but did not) since Emerson too offered a momentary command of existence in subduing his lesser ego to his grand ego. A part of the rather grim comedy of the period of the 1940's and 1950's is that we were in the habit of asking ourselves anxiously why we no longer had political imaginations, political concerns. If we had seen the meaning of our subscription to an iconography of the imagination, we need not have asked these questions. In such art the world has been moved into the self, as in Blake, and the plurality, the inconsequence, the muddiness of existence have been replaced by internalized antinomies. These playlands of the imagination were great fun to explore, but they altogether lacked what a form such as tragedy provides, a recognition that life is actually open-ended. When we come to understand how this cultural shift came about, we will have to admit that while our theory of art ruled out art as a cause, or art as having cognitive value, the theory served simply to protect us from a knowledge of what was happening to our imaginations. As usual in historical matters, we can't tell whether our responsiveness to certain kinds of art was a primary cause, but it is plain that our art and our cultural disposition were after all bound up with one another.

The notion of the impersonality of art became the refuge of the infantile demand to rule the whole world. And with reason. Here after all was a human power one could actually exercise, actually experience. Is there a greater imaginable human power than the power to control the way others apprehend the world? True, it is usually for a moment or a few hours only. But the authority of those hours was not prevented by any theory of art from spilling over into the context of lives. If you can do more living within the palace of art than outside, no discrimination between illusion and reality will still the voice of appetite. Dreams are reality while we dream. Nietzsche would have understood this cultural turn at a glance, though he might have been momentarily puzzled by our failure to see its meaning after he had so harshly warned us of the investments, the personal investments of philosophers in their ostensibly impersonal systems.

I wish to bring the figures I have been discussing together in this chapter, and to indicate the meaning of the welcome they got from us just before and after the middle of the century. It is much easier to do this now than it was only five years ago. The attempt to make art the ark of our humanity is visibly failing. For the young the urgencies and excitements of life are no longer to be found in high culture, and art must play second fiddle to such expressive needs as rock and folk music fulfill. To subdue oneself to art is felt to be almost as much an emotional slavery as to subdue oneself to General Dynamics or the Vietnam war.

To find our way back to a sense of our humanity more inclusive than is provided by art alone is a felt though rather inchoate impulse of the moment. Without pretending to explore the significance of the most recent impulses of youthful disaffiliation, we may find in the groundswell of enthusiasms over the last ten years a number of particular instances. The need the young feel for a total translation of experience, a fresh ground for experience or a new *umwelt* for their sensations, has led to immersion in Tolkien, science fiction, or the substitute world of Blake's prophetic books. The McLuhan vogue penetrated a number of generational levels. It departs from the notion that our sensorium is distorted by print culture, and is but a special case of the excitement provided for the more ambitious by Lévi-Strauss, who has established the intertranslatability of emblems, signs, places, actions as elements of meaning. The leitmotiv appears to be a twin emphasis on the body and language as the frontiers of an exploration of the possibilities of the human animal. Norman O. Brown is of persisting importance as at once agent and emblem of the attempt to reconstruct bodily consciousness. When he fell back from the orgiastic apocalypse to which he points in *Life Against Death*, it was on poetry as the natural word of God, so to speak. In this way he made explicit the nature of the emotional demands that we had been making on art in the period of the new criticism. Even the popular enthusiasm for Robert Ardrey stems from an impulse to find a new base line of human endowment. He has admirers who wish to comprehend a world they sense to be post-social (as well as admirers who wish to defend the status quo by giving it a sanction in a new version of tooth-and-claw Darwinism). Henry Miller is a significant bridging figure, the most forthright of those writers who have seen art as a crutch to be discarded when the imperium of consciousness is truly won. He provides a point of articulation with such figures of the day as Ken Kesey.[2]

Fumbling as these efforts to find a new image of ourselves may be, they suggest that we occupy a cultural position startlingly remote from the period in which we spoke of the artist's "alienation" from society. This opposition was applicable to the modernist tradition which ended with the Second World War, and never had an application to Whitman and Henry James. Our use of it in connection with them is a clear sign of our failure to discriminate the tradition of the imperium of consciousness from the grander tradition of the image described by Frank Kermode in *Romantic Image*. The latter may indeed be past, but Emerson, Whitman, James, the original proponents of the emotional logic we are now employing, are beside us whether we acknowledge them or not. The consciousness these three spoke for was not for a moment ready to see itself as alienated, did not accept the possibility that their world had the power to exclude them. Like the hundreds of thousands who gathered at Woodstock, they saw the demands of society as irrelevant, a very different matter.

Indeed, this is the very root of distinction between Henry James and modernism. He is wholly committed to the triumph of consciousness, to the "obstinate finality" which is his sense of the artist's engagement. This is the reason for his intense and agonized response to the First World War, which took place, as he imagined it, in the

very cathedral of his worship of consciousness. He was no
Yeats to take the "bomb balls" as a recurring affair; no
Lawrence to see in the war a consummation of the surrender to the deadness of mechanism. He had quite simply
counted on the mere existences about him to supply the
conditions which would enable him to make his forms, to
propagate awareness, and they had suddenly let him
down. James seems never to have been cognizant of the
kinds of internal division, in our sense of the world, which
beset Rilke, or Kafka, or Thomas Mann. He had transformed the oppositions and negations in existence into manipulable representations of themselves. When they reas-
serted their original intractability, he was at their mercy.

Something more must be said about modernism and
what is usually felt to be its concomitant, alienation. I
might otherwise seem to be describing a James who was
the complacent laureate of late Victorian and Georgian
times. It was impossible for James, or, I would add, Santayana or George Bernard Shaw, to feel alienated in this
sense, to feel that they had suffered a wound in their very
consciousness of the world because of its indifferent or
brutal response to what they prized. The wounds these
three suffered came earlier, came before they were writers,
and their consequent regression had been matched by a
magnificent power to advance upon the flux of reality and
make it their own. The very price they paid for that power
was the inability to feel that anything was other or alien to
their vision. Theirs may have been a false positive, bitter
alienation a historically more adequate response, but that
is not what needs to be judged here. The fact is that all
three felt that they had found a mode of containing the

world, and that if this was a delusion it was a delusion inextricably wound in the coils of their power.[3]

Both Shaw and James were deeply shaken by the holocaust of the First World War because its universal quality seemed to color the whole imaginative scene. *Heartbreak House* is evidence, as are James's short pieces on the war, that they construed the event as an invasion of their imaginative conditions, a denial of what their very own mastery had achieved. Yet neither changed in a fundamental way. Their modes of taking the world, their versions of consciousness, proved elastic enough to return to much their original set. No such distinctions as those we make between the period of *Hamlet* and *Lear* and that of Shakespeare's romances is applicable to writers such as these. They may well have a succession of adolescences; they cannot have a Sophoclean or Yeatsian development.

Before going any further with James, I ought to remind the reader of the ways in which he is like and unlike my other two imperialists, Emerson and Whitman. James writes of Emerson, "He was in an admirable position for showing, what he constantly endeavored to show, that the prize was within." As the reader knows, I have all along been trying to show how the prize, the whole round world, was moved within in all three figures. The axis of James's moral universe runs (as I showed in *The American Henry James*) from the forms of personal assertion—being a personage (an artifact of class position), possessing goods or esthetic experience, exploiting someone sexually, claiming a special status in the eyes of God or Mrs. Grundy—at one end, to the impersonality of high art or of a selfless and loving generosity at the other end. The parallel axis in

Emerson runs from being a personage on the world's terms, following the rule of expediency or common sense at one end to the impersonality of prophetic vision at the other. What is in each case discovered within the self embraces both extremes, all the appearances are strung on this string. In both men the stick has its shitty end, in each it runs from the appetite to possess or grasp through science or common sense to the hidden divine impulse to see and to celebrate. What is asserted by Emerson and James in common with Whitman is the self that can embrace the world and render it back in visionary utterance in Emerson or in poems and novels in Whitman and James. But James had made the issue between the two loves, the two aspects of the self, the two forms of consciousness the very matter of his greatest drama of consciousness, *The Golden Bowl*, and of this sort of account of the world's claims for itself Emerson's fullest acknowledgment is "Experience," and Whitman's is limited to a single great poem, "Crossing Brooklyn Ferry." But James's partisanship is no less intense for being more variously responsive and more intelligent.

If these are James's judgments of the value of persons, it may still be asked what they have to do with his "grasping imagination." What, as an earnest student once put it, *is* the relationship between love and form in Henry James? The notion of the two loves may be central morally speaking, but what does it have to do with the shape of his fictions? The preceding chapter furnished one major instance of the way in which a novel may be related to James's psychic horizon, his mode of being a nineteenth-century American. I now turn to an answer at once more conventional and more general to the question of the relation of what he loved to what he made. Most generally we are right to say that he loved a world in which things were shaped by mouths in speech, and that which departs from this bears a lesser or an attenuated emotional valence. One of the things which talk handled was sexual behavior, but sexual behavior could never provide an occasion that illuminated the universe of talk. What he could not figure himself as undergoing he was usually too consistent to make more than peripheral for his characters. They could not, for example, be born as Levin's child is born in *Anna Karenina*. Sometimes he makes a revealing slip. Consider the totally unimagined baby attributed to Isabel Archer, a baby who made no ripple in her central consciousness, was in fact a barefaced imaginative cheat from the point of view of those to whom babies actually occur. The Prince and Charlotte could not be lovers except consequentially, that is, the meaning of their being lovers could not be asserted as an experience by itself. In *The Princess Casamassima*, Captain Sholto takes the measure of Hyacinth's splendid abundant shop girl with his eyes; the recorded effect is of Hyacinth's desolation and sense of abandonment. This is not to blind oneself to sexuality but to make it a life-defeating activity which fractures and abridges consciousness. Little Bilham is permitted to refer to the fact that he would have no chance to marry Jeanne de Vionnet in terms of great sexual violence: she won't open to his farthing candle but only to the great golden sun which figures the force of a man of wealth. But the heterosexual force escapes James. Money, the unformed or excreted thing, the other end of the stick of consciousness, has tremendous emotional weight for James. The notion of the penis in the vagina has none. Isabel Archer records a kiss as a lightning flash, but one obviously doesn't live or talk with lightning. James's characters then are just as real as they can talk.

But it is possible to put the matter more generally still. What conditions does Henry James's imagination prescribe for us as readers?

The most direct answer I can think of emerges when we consider why he called the novels of Dostoevsky "fluid puddings." Dostoevsky's characters went about incarnating, manifesting, a series of disparate and even incommensurate inward attitudes, and Dostoevsky freely entered the stream of their preoccupations while allowing them at the same time to enact these preoccupations in the world of the novel's action. All this was presumed to take place on the same fictional plane, just as if, from James's standpoint, a dozen novelists were at work, or as if the world were natively plural. The presence of a dozen "points of view" made for an untidy and cacophonous mess. How could consciousness be plural in its exercise?

The fact that heterosexuality is socialized in Dostoevsky, that sexual emotion is very largely felt on the plane of opposed arguments, of distinctions between poverty and wealth, guilt and innocence, placed Dostoevsky dangerously close to James, and yet very far away: Dostoevsky too was very much a novelist of consciousness, but he produced a world fatally split, in which consciousness could never speak with a single voice, and the archetypal and incessantly threatening crimes were the murder of a father and an assault on a five-year-old girl who—awful and inescapable fact—had a vagina. Such a world was in James's imagination at once uncontrollable and terrifying. A world in which Maisie (of *What Maisie Knew*) is raped, or in which such an event can be imagined, fractures consciousness.

James felt that Dostoevsky's work involved too generous an acceptance of the disparities in people's consciousness of the world as they were revealed in the newspapers, and that this acceptance had led to the creation of a variety of structuring attitudes toward the world of the novel in which his characters were found. Dostoevsky committed an unpardonable sin against consciousness in making characters so authoritative about their own meanings. The primacy of the novelist, the agent of consciousness, who ought to be lord of appearance, was being denied. Balzac was not upsetting in this way because he was, even though naïvely, behind all the appearances; he was omnipresent. The distressing context-ripping, consciousness-multiplying salience of character in Dostoevsky wasn't there in Balzac. Balzac had simply missed the delicious final gesture of imperialism, which was quite to sink yourself in the form, so that your world was only known through what happened in it, and your agency was quite concealed. (I am of course inverting a commonplace here. James didn't bury himself effectually; he can be detected simply because, as we saw in the previous chapter, he had so edited the material that it had always the same gleam, took the chisel in the same way. What this implies about his style, we will come to in a moment.) The appearance on the stage of the novel of more than one shaping intelligence was like giving the show away, not simply as a story, but

as a question of ultimate fictional propriety: it was a mingling of makers with things made.

But can one be to this degree lord of appearance? Yes,
because James was. But what limitations does this lord-
ship entail? I turn for another illustration to a discriminable sort of maker, the maker of symbol and image. Our
most direct sense of these writers is a sense of their triumph in winning the changeless symbol or image from the
world of generation and action. In the absence of the felt
urgencies of being human, of "the foul rag and bone shop
of the heart," they have no force. "Ripeness is all" could
have no meaning in a world of Platonic ideas. James's
world was not to this freezing degree isolated from generation and action. Yet isolated it was, isolated in the precise
measure of his withdrawal from that world. In the measure of that withdrawal the persons encountered in the
world became available as a cast for a cosmic commedia
dell'arte, so many engaged to play the role of wife or child
or Englishman, and all open to his use for a determinate
script, his form. It was the initial unreality of wifehood or
death or being French that made them all available. Indeed, this sense of the unreality of the roles as played in
existence is the node of the relation between the two loves
and form. Sinfulness is identifiable with the esthetic defi-
ciency of believing that your role is absolute, an imaginative stance which denies that life is essentially the creation
of form. To take the form provided by the world's view of
you for a finality is to be at once wholly greedy and the
utter fool of art. By the same reasoning, the only virtue lay
in making forms or loving the makers of forms.

When I was persuaded by Laurence Holland that

James had indeed thought of himself as intimately bound up with Strether, I was at first puzzled.[4] How could he have thought of himself as akin to a man whose defining speech announces that one "takes" the form helplessly, like jelly poured into a mold? The curious love-hate relationship with Strether is, however, wholly and very simply explicable. James is imagining himself as the fool of action; how would it have been to believe that his agency in the world, rather than his agency as creator of forms, was the thing that marked him off? Just as in *The Portrait of a Lady* the bearded young novelist had put on skirts and become the fool of appearance rather than its master, the novelist here leafs out in another possibility: he becomes the moralist in action in the world and meets the exemplary comeuppance of those who take the world of appearance for a finality. (These two novels were described by their writer as his favorites.) To come back to generalities, everybody was either an artist, or a lover of the shaping power, or obversely, a piece of type casting. Consciousness was alone real, but consciousness could find no expression save through the forms it made. (This is an extension of a similar emotional character of Emerson's ruling fantasy: only the particular, myself as seer, can incarnate the general.)

James has then no actual relation to the makers of symbols and images, and what have been called images and symbols in his work may be so called only at the price of an almost complete disjunction from the meanings that attach to these terms when we are discussing Wordsworth or Yeats. This artist does not win through catching up existence into the artifice of eternity: his triumph consists in making the puppets of the cosmic commedia dell'arte speak the lines dictated by the loving consciousness into which they have been incorporated. "Let us treat the men and women well; treat them as if they were real," said Emerson, "perhaps they are." [5] But of course they aren't. And what Emerson is finally saying is, entertain them if they don't propose themselves as hopelessly dialectic finalities. For Emerson and James alike the Pauline exhortation against a "respect of persons" was in fact gospel. It sometimes reaches a paradigmatic extremity in James, as in *The Awkward Age*, in which the game of slipping from one center of consciousness to another is played with an uncannily single-minded self-absorption using a set of puppets almost uniformly contemptible, whose very triviality serves to highlight the game itself. Instead of "button, button," it is "who has the illuminating candle in the scene at hand"?

We may now say something about the most inclusive of the effects of James's prose. It is so pervasive as to escape direct remark, and it is refracted in objections to the late style, or objections to the claustral character of his work, or objections to his tendency to write about the upper classes exclusively. We may put it shortly by saying that in James words and phrases don't assume an independent resonance. This may sound like a way of saying that he isn't a poet, but it is more than that. There is no passage in James that has the sudden authority of dream reference, there is no element of strength that is not subdued to the form—in fact, when you find a passage that is not, you have found weakness, not strength, in the work at hand. Like the search for an Emersonian esthetic, symbol-

hunting in James is not only useless but altogether misleading because it tends to impose the notion that particular works have been won from the world of generation and
action apprehended by the writer. But the material never
presented that initial difficulty, and the kind of resonance
which follows from making the unchanging thing that
represents the changing world cannot therefore be found
in James's fiction. What is found is the play of consciousness of which the world is but the ostensible show, the
manifestation insofar as it is consciousness. James's works,
or, he assumes, the works of anybody who can actually
write or paint or act or sculpt are felt to be the real thing,
the sum of being. Simple organisms, the buzz of existence,
these are merely stuff offered to the writer, *prima materia.*
Expressive form is being, and words cannot have a bright
singularity because—as the Prince says to Charlotte, "a
ricordo from you—from you to me—is a *ricordo* of
nothing," that is, what has *happened* between us is
nothing.[6] The image and the symbol are literary ways of
making human action and its conditions present in consciousness; since for James human action *consists* in the
recorded play of consciousness, they refer to nothing independent of the fabric of the work itself. Of course, it follows that a character who spoke with a Dickensian dis-
tinctness would tear that fabric; they must all sound more
or less like the master.

The emphasis I have made on the characterization of
Dostoevsky's novels as "fluid puddings," my insistence
that James perceived his world along an oral-anal axis
(what isn't formed is excremental), may, together with
the assertion that the distinction of sex and the finalities of

the human condition were softened and transformed into manipulable elements, the scene and the cast of a cosmic commedia dell'arte, be taken to mean that James was somehow emotionally effete or dead, that he did not feel the force of existence but handled it with tongs and at a fatal remove. This would amount to saying that James had no emotional investments of a compelling sort. The case is very much the reverse. James, I must insist, was indeed a passionate man, a passionate writer, and to discriminate the objects of his attention and the character of his attention to the world is my affair, not to deny the intensity of his absorption in it. We all translate existence into our own terms; this is not a way of judging the quantum of our capacity to feel. The empire of the self in James was not ruled by a passionless intelligence.

As among Emerson, Whitman, and James, the completeness with which impersonality proclaimed the hidden demand for a complete imaginative conquest of existence was of course distinct in measure, partly distinct in kind. Emerson's audience remained in part a congregation, and in this degree he was less susceptible to immersion in his own verbal artifacts; since he was less hidden in his maker's cloud, he made a lesser claim on his audience. But the endless struggle in the journals to make the universe sound his note qualifies our sense of him, even though it was not a part of the experience of his contemporaries. In the case of Whitman we cannot speak of a single structuring point of view for each of his works, nor was his need of such ordering so extortionate; he was in public possession of his body as ground of being, while James's body is present but as the sound box of his speech, and the shadowy anus is focused only occasionally as the source of the bad, the dull, the unformed or the malign forces in his world, as it is when Nanda Brookenham speaks of herself as a pipe through which filth flows, and remarks that "it sticks to us."

Each of the three was committed by his very perspective on the world to the reduction, the editing, of the sensibility of audience or reader; each was aware that the axes of the selves they confronted must be repolarized; that every member of the putative audience must be persuaded to abandon the middle ground for the inward empire in which assumptions about the world, horizontal relationships, counted not as limiting data but only as material for the self.

But the three must be distinguished with respect to what initially offered itself as material as well. Chronologically, we get a quickly ascending curve of inclusiveness. For Emerson the materials to be dealt with were in some ways very limited indeed. Beginning with the self which found itself sundered, role-encumbered, unfathered, islanded by nothingness, at one extreme, and imperial, free of time and circumstance at the other, Emerson was condemned to say one thing endlessly. His genius lay in his use of the texture of language, the texture of allusion, the familiar uses of words. The resistance he encountered and overcame lay precisely in verbal habit and conventional expectation, which he forever defeats by making the language, all chopped up as it is by the fragmented concerns of newspapers and novels and patent-medicine ads, the whole variety of social uses we find for it, hum to one tone, or play variations on his imperial theme. He subdued the multitudinous world by subduing the lexical elements to himself.

Whitman too was engaged in a "language experiment," to quote one of his suppositions about what he was up to in *Leaves of Grass*. To make his body and the delightful feats of his sensorium central he had to swallow up things and persons into processes and flows and movements till all the world swirled around him. Of course he often visibly sweats at the job. (He is never finally clear whether he wants to be loved as a poem or loved as Walt.) In him what Norman O. Brown calls the *"causa sui* project" is more explicit than in Emerson. It approaches the condition of drama:

> *It is time to explain myself—let us stand up.*[7]

—a line in which the association of movement with a deliverance of the total intention is not in the least inconsequent. In Whitman the feebleness of such cant phrases of our time as "telling it like it is," and being "with it," and "in the groove," and "heavy" (for deeply felt), which are no more than the shibboleths that mark off a tract of feeling on the grounds of its intensity and total disconnection from those complexes of emotion associated with the rejected society, is replaced by the imaginative project of conveying just such feelings with as much of their fullness as the poet can muster. There is no hint of the objective correlative, only the direct effort to induce inclusive sensations and penumbras of awareness. The calamus root and the live oak are not things out there but are themselves "uttered" as is Whitman, incitements to a like sense of process and growth:

The efflux of the soul is happiness, here is happiness,
I think it pervades the open air, waiting at all times,
Now it flows unto us, we are rightly charged.

Here rises the fluid and attaching character,
The fluid and attaching character is the freshness and
sweetness of man and woman,
(The herbs of the morning sprout no fresher and sweeter
every day out of the roots of themselves, than it
sprouts fresh and sweet continually out of itself.)
Toward the fluid and attaching character exudes the
sweat of the love of young and old,
From it falls distilled the charm that mocks beauty and
attainments,
Toward it heaves the shuddering longing ache of contact.
                                   (*"Song of the Open Road"*)

Whitman is not accessible to the vocabularies ordinarily
employed in criticism because these cannot deal with an
exhibition of the *causa sui* project. If we say of Emerson
that he used his capacity to break down the ordinary discriminations language makes to further his imperialism,
we must say that Whitman invites language to participate
in its own dissolution. In the passage I have just quoted
nothing is newly named, it is the very reverse of the
Adamic, what is happening to the words is that they are
being sacrificed to the job of pointing beyond themselves
to unnamable qualities of experience. In such a language
general terms have a greater specificity than particulars in
the degree that they bring us closer to the dissolution of
the conventional perspectives of experience:

Who is he that would become my follower?
Who would sign himself a candidate for my affection?

The way is suspicious, the result uncertain, perhaps
destructive,
You would have to give up all else, I alone would expect
to be your sole and exclusive standard,
Your novitiate would even then be long and exhausting,
The whole past theory of your life and all conformity to
the lives around you would have to be
abandon'd . . .

         (*"Whoever You Are Holding Me Now in Hand"*)

What lies just beyond the greatest of imaginable Whitman poems is completely in accord with Henry Miller's forecast of the state in which art will no longer be necessary: a shout in the street will indeed fill the sky vacated by the god.

These comments on the uses of language in the three writers under discussion which most clearly reflect the *causa sui* project are of course incomplete. When James is writing about Balzac or Chartres, or New England's light and seascapes, he is an extraordinarily gifted recorder of the shapes and qualities of things. He chose to subordinate this gift very firmly to that of the maker of forms. We might put it that for James there is no real tension between things observed and things made because they shared equally in the fate of being known to him. Of course, this is the very thing that does set off the writers in Kermode's tradition of the image. To win things from time and change, to make a changeless record of the consequences of time and change, is just their concern. The almost unthinkably ahistorical character of Emerson, Whitman, and James is a part of the tradition of consciousness which cannot entertain the notion of an internal division brought about by time. The author of *The Sense of the Past* had no sense of the past for the very reason that he could not assume a generational place, had no rooted loyalty to a particular culture, and therefore had to do all the work of being human for himself. Perhaps no one really chooses the elements which a personality such as James's stitches into a world. But the assumption everywhere is that from the moment he was able to do so he chose, he saw, and he recorded and created at the command of his own imagination. Leon Edel records an instance of his deleting a trip to Europe on the part of the family from his memoirs. Apparently it simply seemed incoherent!

Finally we must speak not simply of how he shapes things for others in his works, his letters, his notes for himself, his travel books, his conversation, and so on, but how he has all along been receiving what he shaped. Nothing is more often before us in the memoirs than this: that he was all the while taking things in, taking them as they came, and that there was an accretion of things taken in, and that some had been marked, had had a red-letter sharpness or a categorical inclusiveness, but had only been marked as of an order of importance, not as disjunctions, breaks, total, to use a term of which James was, oddly enough, fond, "transformation scenes." What the small scared consciousness had caught up, it had caught up for the man of seventy. One is reminded of the nineteenth-century fantasy about our knowledge, our scientific knowledge of the world. It was a plane on which we planted flags at ever greater distance from the starting point, the center, and as we conquered the plain so our knowledge grew in wider circles of generality inclusive of more and more recorded evidence about the nature of things. We have the greatest difficulty in taking this in: for Henry James consciousness was one, the dream was mastered. That quality of distinctiveness which may attach to each of the recorded bits of awareness was never of such a character that it could not be strung on the web; whatever could not be strung did not for its purposes exist. Thus, it is precisely the same quality which makes James endlessly fascinating to some persons that also makes him unbearably boring to others. Those for whom it is an endless delight to participate in the activities of an endlessly responsible consciousness must either be very strong to bear the weight of its implication of an unbroken world, or be very much subject to precisely the most inclusive of all human delusions, that everything, beauty, detail, persons, horror, disjunction, death, may be acknowledged by the undivided consciousness. It is perhaps no accident that James's biographer might be called the "man without ironies," and that many of his most enchanted commentators have shared the sense that the world had best be taken as form, because it otherwise presents divisions and blanks and functions they cannot bear to contemplate simultaneously.

The dream can be mastered; the dream cannot be mastered, this is but one way of putting our disjunction as to attitudes toward James as they appear in particular men. Another way is of course to say that there either is or is not a consciousness such that it belies the human situation in a primary way. Mastery of the dream, any dream, would mean that we could finish analyzing it, that we could make one story of it. Much the same thing may be said of the products of the undivided consciousness, the intending undivided consciousness, that it makes of the scene of human agency one story, that it knows too much. But this is really the same thing as saying that the dream can be mastered. Whatever the situation in the eyes of a posited all-knower, our own situation is one in which the beset cerebrum can never say that it has mastered what is without any more than it has mastered what issues from within. To report what one has seen of the world, or to write stories about it in which the assumption of mastery is made and our incomplete mastery is in no way a part of the process, is to be a "beautiful author." But, we reply, he does it as he saw it! Yes, and what he didn't see was the incompleteness. There the question rests, and it isn't properly to be pursued here, since as thus proposed it is a moral question, and we have been employing historical categories.

James is unlike Emerson and Whitman in that he admits and even brilliantly describes a various and voluminous world. But he is no less rigorous than they in making it submit to his own imaginative order. All three imaginations are so commanding, tend so much to incorporation, that we may properly speak of them as performing a function for their possessors analogous to that of a religion in other men. In all three the compelling character of history, generational order, places and things leaches out, tends to disappear. Those emotional returns which in order of magnitude, and in terms of the quantum of assurance they provide, are comparable to the returns of religious faith, would not be available to these men in a world heavily qualified by time and place. As we noted in connection with Emerson, they could not bear the sense of psychic diminution which sonship imposed on them. Better far to be a son of one's works, an Emerson bent over a journal, a Whitman revising *Leaves of Grass*, a James elaborating a splendid shell for himself in The New York Edition, than to be pinned by the urgencies and anomalies of a historical moment. The world must submit to me on my terms.

Still another way of suggesting the quality of the life and work of these sons of the undivided consciousness is to recall how unremitting was the business of being Emerson, Whitman, or Henry James in daily life. When Henry James is reseeing (rather than revising) his work, he evokes a delighted self-approbation and an occasional ruefulness in himself that reminds us of Whitman lounging and admiring himself in *Leaves of Grass*. Both may remind us of Emerson at work within himself, conning the journals for the passages which would provide the ostensible particulars of an essay. The beautifully articulated personal presences that were theirs are a part of the world's testimony about them. (Allen Ginsberg is a modern avatar of this unremitting attention to producing that presence which establishes an unbroken continuity between the man and his work.) When Henry James encountered a friend or wrote a letter, he was all there; he was there as the maker. Who else was there to be? Dickens, Dostoevsky, Conrad, Balzac are very far off when we look at the spectacle which was James-and-his-work. The muddy, the inconclusive, the frantic, the publicly exultant or publicly despairing, the—in a word—*transitive* character of these lives was not his. He was simply the agent of his unresting consciousness. He seems made to order for the phenomenological critic who will proceed to treat his whole career as one imaginative act, one inclusive paradigm, itself seen as constitutive of the historical moment of its appearance. Separate works, internal anomalies, biographical and cultural breaks, defeats, potentialities, all will be smoothed into the printed corpus: the verbal artifact is all.

To push James to this logical limit is to remind ourselves of the counter figure, Hawthorne, that imperfect artist, whose imperfection Trilling sees as connected with his humanity, that of a man who knew that art was not and could not be all.[8] His denunciation of the "mystic sensuality of this singular age" and of a kind of egoism recognizably "transcendental" is so central a response to the impulses manifested in Emerson, Whitman, and Henry James that I must return to it here. What Hawthorne was troubled by is related to Herbert Marcuse's nightmare of the materialization of ideals in an industrial society, or the linguistic phenomenon of closure, which is said to forestall the statement of potentialities, unrealized possibilities.[9] Emerson's mingling of the immediate and the prospective murders time and kidnaps ideals, originally nursed in the manifold culture, into the imperium of the self. Once inside they have no future which is not that of the self, and no past because, as I have said perhaps too often, the imperial self will not tolerate the notion of its genesis through growth. We may say this in a way which brings us closer to Hawthorne's terms: the transcendental egoist transforms his relations with others because he is canted toward the future. This drains his present relationships of that constitutive meaning they had for Hawthorne. And the future itself is not the collective future of Christian hope, but the future posited by the self. Is the future the future if it is only yours, or if the presence of others in it is subject to

Emerson's detached anticipation that "we shall meet again on a higher platform"?

Hawthorne saw as radically identical the act of detaching yourself from your fellows and the act of appropriating material things and other men for a use you declared morally and spiritually preeminent. His description of Hollingsworth in *The Blithedale Romance* shows what a gothic horror this had for him:

> This is always true of those men who have surrendered themselves to an overruling purpose. It does not so much impel them from without, nor even operate as a motive power within, but grows incorporate with all that they think and feel, and finally converts them into little else save that one principle. When such begins to be the predicament, it is not cowardice, but wisdom to avoid these victims. They have no heart, no sympathy, no reason, no conscience. They will keep no friend, unless he make himself the mirror of their purpose; they will smite and slay you, and trample your dead corpse under foot, all the more readily, if you take the first step with them, and cannot take the second, and the third, and every other step of their terribly strait path. They have an idol to which they consecrate themselves high-priest, and deem it holy work to offer sacrifices of whatever is most precious; and never once seem to suspect—so cunning has the Devil been with them—that this false deity, in whose iron features, immitigable to all the rest of mankind, they see only benignity and love, is but a spectrum of the very priest himself, projected

upon the surrounding darkness. And the higher and purer the original object, and the more unselfishly it may have been taken up, the slighter is the probability that they can be led to recognize the process by which godlike benevolence has been debased into all-devouring egotism.[10]

Hawthorne's darkness was Emerson's and Whitman's light. The romancer was incapable, as are people who conceive their human world as made up of a network of relationships among persons, of seeing self-absorption as anything other than a lurid social fact, an immediate danger to those with whom the egotist was involved. That he saw the cranks and visionaries who were attracted to Emerson as just such persons as Hollingsworth is clear, but precisely because he could not imagine the Emersonian absorption in self as other than actively malign—as directed against others—he could not see the more frightening fact about it, that it involved the withdrawal of affect on the part of many persons, all who were willing to listen, from the whole nexus of human relationships. He could not see, for instance, that Emerson's essay "Friendship" is a more disturbing testimony to the moribund condition of community than the appearance of such an obsessed creature as Hollingsworth.

We get a sharper juxtaposition with Emerson when we consider the situation Hawthorne imagined in creating little Pearl. She is precisely the enforced transcendentalist, the human being deprived of the sustaining relationships which foster human selves. The vivid assertiveness of this infant isolato gives us the measure of Hawthorne's power to imagine the unfathered Emersonian self. Like Hollingsworth, she has one fixed idea, in her case clearly imposed from without; the letter is her enforced obsession. She is always asking, What does it mean and how does it discriminate me from the rest of the world? She is an imagined case of human isolation, beautiful, witty, inhuman, cold, but free of the intent to destroy attributed to Hollingsworth, untouched by the hate which is transformed love, the love which is transformed hate, which ties Dimmesdale to Chillingworth. Their energies flow from their investment in others; Pearl is pinned to her obsession: How to transform the sign which organizes the whole world of her perceptions into life? A late Emerson passage, very clear-cut as to the *causa sui* project, provides what we may call a positive rendering of the plight of the isolated self to pose against the situation of little Pearl:

> The height of culture, the highest behavior, consists in the identification of the ego with the universe; so that when a man says, I hope, I find, I think, he might properly say, the human race finds or thinks or hopes. And meantime he shall be able continually to keep sight of his biographical Ego,—I have a desk, I have an office, I am hungry, I had an ague,—as rhetoric or offset to his grand spiritual Ego, without impertinence, or ever confounding them.[11]

It is more than convenient that Emerson should refer to this mad endeavor as "the height of culture"; it serves to make explicit his rejection of what we now think of as culture, that filiation of memory, custom and expectation, articulate and tacit, which binds a human generation in a humanly qualified place and leads its members to act in describable roles. In this passage the translation of the attempt to become one with God into that of assimilation of the whole, voice of the whole, is also declared and open. For all such endeavors Hawthorne's contempt and loathing is obvious. The plurality of our obligations, their recurrent incompatibility, and the demand that we love our fellows as ourselves were inescapable for him.

On the basis of the results achieved in the last generation the study of American literature has been rather more effective in obscuring our understanding of American culture than in furthering it. We have learned a good deal about our texts at the price of an almost complete divorce of the texts from an imagined set of makers and readers. The circumstantial scholarship of American studies has been of marginal usefulness. The chief thrust of literary criticism has been to substitute an account of how works gave birth to works under the aegis of symbol or myth or the awareness of human depravity or mechanism or what not for the endeavor to find the human locus of imaginative accomplishment on a scene the historian could conceivably recognize. Given the relative thinness and fragmentation which characterize our provincial nineteenth century, it may be intelligible that we succumbed to the impulse to make its literary artifacts support themselves and each other in a historical void, but our present cultural circumstances have exposed the impossibility of continuing to do so. If in the absence of other things an Emerson

filled the vacancy between heaven and earth with his assertion, we had better find ways of recognizing the meaning
of impulses which transcend symbol-hunting and analyses
of literary forms.

At the moment the interesting work seems most likely to
come from the historians who concern themselves with the
relation of character structure and familial relationships to
culture. But we cannot content ourselves with one methodology. It may emerge that anthropology is even more helpful. For instance, Lévi-Strauss's "models of diversity"
might prove useful on more limited time scales than he
employs. It is not simply law or literary works or dress or
architecture that carry the burden of meaning for human
beings. We have to learn to read between the cultural
lines, and find paradigms expressive of tracts of evidence
about ourselves now missing. But this kind of endeavor is
in the future. What lies behind has to be reckoned with
too, in particular the work of our first intellectual historian
of real distinction, Perry Miller. Any consideration of such
questions as What made Emerson possible? must still
begin with him.

Miller's biography of Jonathan Edwards makes one assertion which, if accepted, would surely be axial to our cultural history. It is maintained that Edwards substituted individual experience for authority in validating the whole
Christian mythos. I don't mean that Edwards is said to
have believed that there was a choice for the individual
Christian, but that Miller sees him as saying that the
whole of the Christian tradition must be reexperienced,
undergone by, each believer, whose exercise of his own
wits, his own sensibility, thus became primary.

Miller's virtuosity in making a coherent drama out of the seventeenth century's attempt to found the city on the hill and of its failure was supplied with a third act of an almost too tempting elegance and inclusiveness by the Edwards whom he describes. But some recent research (for example, Richard Bushman's *From Puritan to Yankee*) makes it appear that Edwards does indeed represent a shift in the base of authority detectable in many of Connecticut's New Lights; that we may with some plausibility think of them as lying behind Emerson's use of the primacy of the individual mind as the arbiter of value and truth. This is a commonplace, but a commonplace which has been glossed over. (Human beings are now demanding the counterpart of Christian beatitude as a natural right; in these circumstances the origins of these gigantesque claims for the self become of acute interest.)

In one obvious way Miller must be distinguished from a later generation of scholars. His analytic tools were, first, a keen sense of the intention which lay behind the reworking of systems of thought through which each generation sought to make inherited structures amenable to its needs; second, a comprehensive grasp of the paradigms which were subject to change—often, it appears, more comprehensive than that attributable to any of those who subscribed to them. His *Jonathan Edwards* simply outpaces by miles any other biography of an American thinker: it is really difficult, really profound, in its effort to assess the relations between the man and his ideas. It has not been coped with by its critics on the level of its own range and seriousness. But what Miller notably lacked was a nose for those qualities in thought and language which reflect the dream state, the kind of perception that Nietzsche had of the oppositions, doublenesses, contradictions, and condensations that find their way into systems of thought and into attempts to change them. He was innocent, for example, of what a good many historians of culture now posit without always being explicit about it: the psychic need manifested by a particular generation. Insofar as it found verbal expression, he could handle it brilliantly; if it did not, his method failed to lay hold on it. His later work is often vitiated because he depended too much upon the discovery of an implicit paradigm in instances in which what he had to cope with was not so much a verbal order as an emotional demand, which did not find expression in words but in other forms of behavior. The upshot was that he could not make the transition from Edwards to Emerson in a convincing way, and that his treatment of American "romanticism"—a questionable concept to begin with— marked as always by extraordinarily wide learning, isn't really illuminating.[12] Just in the measure perhaps that Jonathan Edwards's use of his version of the authority of experience made intellectual structures secondary to individual testimony, diminishing the stress of passion which the intellect had earlier carried, so does the later work of Miller fail to lay hold of the cultural history of the later period with the authority he shows in dealing with what happened up to the 1740's.

That diminution in stress is not of course present in Edwards himself; in what seems to us his greatest work, *Treatise Concerning the Religious Affections*, it is precisely the intellectual fervor with which he hunts down and elegantly discriminates the passions that engages us.

Miller and others have been able to point to a bifurcation of attention to things which were united in Edwards, and to speak of traditions of rational religion and revivalism as both issuing from Edwards. This distinction has, however, tended to obscure something of importance, if the conclusions of this essay are sound. The account now traditional posits an increasingly dull and rationalistic religious strain that amounts to a progressive secularization: religion as a principle of public order, ethical regulation, justification for the status quo. This is thought of as provoking a reaction among those who become known as transcendentalists, a recurrence to Anne Hutchinson's claim to private judgment bolstered by Coleridge and German idealism is thought of as lying behind the impulses of the transcendentalists and other come-outers of the 1830's and 1840's. Without diminishing the importance of Coleridge and the rest, we must note a suspicious taint of faculty psychology in the original disjunction between revivalism and rational religion, and ask whether my treatment of Emerson does not provide some ground for treating transcendentalism not simply as a reaction to the pale negations of Boston Unitarianism, but as a reaction to the lapsing away of certain supportive structures in American culture as well. To do so engages us with a more modern psychology in which the disappearance of the society of deference and the coming of Jacksonianism appear momentous emotionally as well as in the ways we are accustomed to think them so. In this context, Richard Hofstadter's remark that transcendentalism sometimes appears to have been the revivalism of the intellectuals[13] takes on additional force, and the emphasis on the revivals in

Miller's posthumously published work seems sound and worth carrying further.[14] The emotional concomitants of Jacksonianism comprise, it seems to me, a highly promising subject for historical research.

To rehearse this from a different angle: it has all along been conventional to assume what New England's seventeenth- and eighteenth-century preachers did: that people had turned to the loves of the world and the flesh. But nothing we have learned about our nature in the epoch of depth psychology shows that there is much point to thinking that the result was a class of pleasure-loving vs. a class of virtue-pursuing persons. To follow out the logic in this way is to turn hortatory terms into analytic ones, and —as it happened—to give Marxist notions the place formerly occupied by the contention of the preachers that people had turned simply to acquisition. Neither the Marxist notions nor the positing of sheer acquisitiveness lay hold of the problem posed by the appearance of the imperial self— a self which assumed psychic burdens because outer supportive structures of custom and institutions had disappeared or lost imaginative authority.[15]

To think of the generation of Emerson's father as sunk in the mores of State Street is not wrong, but is clearly inadequate as an explanation of their relative spiritual sloth. May we not suppose that they enjoyed sources of emotional assurance that Emerson found lacking? To do so is to grant them a full humanity once more; our present version of them reduces them to figures in a cartoon.

I return, then, to the suggestion advanced earlier in this essay: Americans appear to have suffered a punishing psychic blow in the generation of Emerson's youth, to have lost the assurance provided by their sense of the presence of leaders and an instituted order. Revivalism may well have been employed to cope with this, although this isn't a sufficient account of revivalism. But the New England ferment of the epoch of the Chardon Street Convention, which was produced by the members of Emerson's own generation, is at once a more imaginative and a more desperate response to the situation I have posited. Such a book as Fred Somkin's *Unquiet Eagle* is worth a good deal of attention.[16] He provides evidence that about Lafayette's triumphal progress through the states in the mid-'twenties it may be said that it provoked a curious double response on the part of those who did the welcoming. First, Lafayette was indeed a revered founding father; second, the sons had somehow absorbed the power and authority he had manifested as one of their creators into themselves. What had been done originally by individuals was now in some unexplained way being manifested by the collectivity, the new nation, or, and this is the point I should make, had become available, like the shaman's mana, to each of those who dwelt in the new nation. Somkin's thesis is that the welcome to Lafayette involved an unconscious attempt to reconstitute the sacred community in the presence of forces, chiefly prosperity (acquisitiveness again!), which served to break it down. I question this. The nation was still so new when it lost its sense of its original character that the notion of breaking the sacred bond seems far-fetched. Had there been three generations of the heroic mold followed by a marked and acknowledged decline, one might be able to follow Somkin in thinking of the country as subject to the rises and falls commonly attributed to successive dynasties of greater and lesser heroic virtue. But in this case the nation was not much more than a generation old when it appeared to have stepped out of time, if we may put it so. The national focus was no longer apparent, and the movement from the society of deference to the society of the political caucus, borrowing Fischer's terms, represented so complete a change in the sense of how society was ordered that it felt like a qualitative break, not simply an increase in the people's influence over national affairs.[17] But these are issues the historians must reckon with.

For the purposes of my essay, I simply assert that Emerson became "Emerson" in a period in which there was an acute and widely diffused emotional demand for a new mode of self-validation. We may also remark that the mode Emerson found answers in more than the commonplace ways to the demand. If many people had found it unusually easy to come by a competence, if many had found that they could in some way count, if there had indeed been an emotional leveling up as well as a political one, if (to recall the contention of *Plainville, U.S.A.*),[18] we have indeed long expected so much of our children as to cast our fatherhood into the shade, there was an emotional logic about the assertion that each man was gifted with an infinite potential, precisely because he was father to himself, had in some measure been influenced by the view of the world which Brown calls the *causa sui* project.

The loss sustained had been of the assurance provided by a sense of who stood above and who below in the scale; the appropriate remedy appears to have been the proclamation that the scale itself was incorporated within each man, who ranged from his petty personal ego to his "grand spiritual Ego." That this hunger which I am presuming Emerson satisfied was stilled in another fashion by evangelical religion we find it easy to believe, since we have all along thought of the revival as an occasion for social as well as religious reaffirmation of sonship and brotherhood. What has been lacking is some sketch of the emotional returns Emerson and his congeners offered. These, if my thesis is correct, have turned out in the long run to be vastly more influential than what revivalism offered.

Since the term "consciousness" isn't quite available to set alongside the tradition of image and symbol I have compared with it, and since that self which catches up a whole world including a scale encompassing the thing denied at one end and the imperial affirmation at the other also fails of parallelism, how can we name the American version of the tradition I have been writing about? The world literally in the self is a description of madness, and my theme is not madness; rather a species of enforced retreat from the world in which selves had been realized on a transitive basis. And clearly only a partial retreat. These shifts from communal modes of self-validation to a psychic self-reliance have always been a part of magic and religion, and perhaps of action itself. It is not only true that Napoleon isn't crazy if he thinks he is Napoleon; it is also true that Napoleon had to be a little crazy to think he could become Napoleon. "All mortal greatness is but disease," says Ahab. The most suggestive and least misleading term I can offer is "incorporation."

Incorporation can hardly be thought of as more than predominant in any given case. We cannot say of Hawthorne that his fidelity to the ideal of community was absolute. The projection of communal hope in *Blithedale* is touched with despair, while Emerson's assertion of an imperial selfhood had to be endlessly repeated and often gives way in late work to an effort to socialize individual powers.

Yet the two impulses are clearly discriminable, and the future historian of our letters will be constrained to find a way of understanding them which is apprehensible to historians. He will also have to reckon with the cultural meaning of our enthusiasm for Henry James and Whitman in the period just preceding our own. The effort to rest the sanctions of morality on the creative imagination expressed in works in which the chief sin is to accept a social role or a sexual role as given was a cultural symptom of high importance. In the universe constituted by *The Golden Bowl* the human givens which made for epic, tragedy, the transcendent God, politics, and the imaginative recognition of such commonplaces as birth, parenthood, and death are all swallowed up. There is no escaping it: if you master all you know and feel you can only play the universal role, you are your absolute.

The methodology of such historical investigations as this essay suggests must, I think, involve the recognition that we assume varying cultural burdens from generation to generation, which is to say no more than that if the making of selves varies so does the scene on which they move, and that the ties imaginatively loosened by one generation may be knit up by a subsequent generation in a distinct way.

I also believe that literature will have to be brought within the circle of historical concerns in a fresh mode. Our nineteenth-century literature made an exploration of kinds of consciousness minimally supported by cultural sanctions. These subsequently flowered in European writing, but we appear to have become the innovators once more in the degree to which we have found modes of acting out, rather than simply being an audience for, the post-social fantasies of a Whitman.

That acting out, that refusal of the differenced roles, is now widespread. "All separate identities are bankrupt," writes Allen Ginsberg. In writing this book I have assumed for expository ends the underlying constancy of the separate identities and of the grown up or genital character, while noting that it found expression in differing ways. (Hawthorne was able to establish the fatality of sexual role in the terms his cultural moment afforded.) The assumption of this underlying constancy is in part simply methodologically convenient. Employing it, I was able to show that Emerson's blurring of the immediate and the prospective is not simply an assault on the self reciprocally known; it murders time and kidnaps ideals into the single consciousness, destroying their character of shared hope. It also enabled me to show that Whitman's all-engrossing consciousness is based on a body reshaped to its uses, and that Henry James's "point of view" is in the first instance the psychic necessity of the undivided consciousness, since all the differenced roles were equally unreal, equally available as material. For him such created forms as *The Golden Bowl* were the necessary containers of consciousness; Allen Ginsberg and his fellows have moved beyond them into a consciousness which uses, but is not contained by, forms—life is a "harmless emptiness" in Ginsberg's marvelous phrase.[19]

I have all along been aware of the irony implicit in my enterprise: my contemporaries show a strong impulse to step out of time and the constraints of associated life; I have been explaining that Emerson was their predecessor (ancestor is impossible in this context)—in the process I am enacting the role of the time-bound nineteenth-century European. Such a passage as the one below—from the third paragraph of Emerson's first book, *Nature* (1836) —tempts us to feel that the whole nineteenth-century adventure with time, the character of history as we have understood it, of society as we have understood it, even the assumption of new yet fatal roles as givens, which we call "romanticism," was an episode on the surface:

> But to a sound judgment, the most abstract truth is the most practical. Whenever a true theory appears it will be its own evidence. Its test is, that it will explain all the phenomena. Now many are thought not only unexplained but inexplicable; as language, sleep, madness, dreams, beasts, sex.

To most of Emerson's literate contemporaries this use of "sound judgment" and its association with an "abstract truth" which was at the same time "the most practical" was dithering, sound without sense. We have no such assurance. It is pretty clear that if we were to summon a convocation of intellectuals in 1970 they would invoke, as Emerson does, the supreme authority of consciousness (a presentment which is "its own evidence"), and that they would draw up much the same list of things to be explained. Emerson proposes this list as problematic because those matters which his contemporaries would have proposed, did propose, were all fatally transitive, public, like politics and temperance. In short, the whole nineteenth-century taste for purposeful change is secondary or accidental in Emerson's imagination, just as it is to so many around us.

But of course I have no intention of closing my Hegel, Marx, Nietzsche, Freud, and opening my Boehme, Blake, Frye, and Ginsberg. The figures in nineteenth- and twentieth-century American writing who, with the exception of Hawthorne, have been neglected in this book— Cooper, Melville, Twain, Faulkner, Hemingway—comprise the tradition which engages my sympathies. Leslie Fiedler's refusal (in *Love and Death in the American Novel*) to grant Hawthorne, Cooper, Melville, and Twain a certificate of Oedipal resolution is ahistorical, a piece of Oedipal selfrighteousness. Their struggles do indeed attest to the difficulty of growing up in this country—but what nation had ever gone so far toward dissolving social ties as this one? Melville's magnificent power to negate, as in *Bartleby*, is witness to his power to affirm: to hurl that harpoon—a power denied to the all-engrossing selves who are forever saying yes to the world they have identified with the content of their very own consciousness.

Having sketched the habit of incorporation in Emerson, Whitman, and James, I wish to make a final contrast between the two imaginative modes, that of incorporation and that of agency. Suppose we drop what has been methodologically convenient, the assumption of constancy on the part of genital or transitive character? D. H. Lawrence tacitly did so when he described these two imaginative modes in *Studies in Classic American Literature* in 1922. I quote first three passages from his description of the habit of incorporation in Whitman, which, he declares, had to fail because of the nature of things:

> The difference between life and matter is that life, living things, living creatures, have the instinct of turning right away from *some* matter, and of blissfully ignoring the bulk of most matter, and of turning towards only some certain bits of specially selected matter. . . . Your mainspring is broken Walt Whitman. The mainspring of your own individuality. And so you run down with a great whirr, merging with everything.
>
> Walt wasn't an esquimo. A little yellow, sly, cunning greasy little Esquimo. And when Walt blandly assumed Allness, including Esquimoness, unto himself, he was just sucking the wind out of a blown eggshell, no more. Esquimos are not minor little Walts. I know that. Outside the egg of my Allness chuckles the greasy little Esquimo. Outside the egg of Whitman's Allness too.

This is what I called the "hypertrophied self" in discussing Emerson and James in *The American Henry James*. Lawrence's characterization of our tradition of agency, based chiefly on his reading of Cooper, is no less pejorative, and it is now an article of faith among some American intellectuals: "The essential American soul is hard, isolate, lonely, stoic, and a killer." [20] Lawrence was wrong

about one thing; Whitman seems to me to have had a re-
sounding success in diffusing his consciousness. But was
Lawrence enjoying a prevision of the fate of genitality in
this country? *Why Are We in Vietnam?* is a novel whose
very title proclaims it a proposition in cultural history.
Norman Mailer's tenderness for the basis of communal life
has gone to lengths which may seem extravagant. He is,
for example, deeply distrustful of contraception because it
robs sexual intercourse of its dialectical and sequential
meaning, takes it out of biological time into some infantile
eternity. The whole body of his work speaks to the necessity of the differenced roles and, like the somewhat muted
voice of Saul Bellow, is an affirmation much fuller than
Hawthorne's of the self reciprocally known. So it is shaking to find him saying with Lawrence that genitality has
been assimilated to the impulse to kill. If incorporation be-
gets nothing and genitality is indeed isolate, our image is
of an insular Tahiti of orality and the penis transformed
into a weapon—both encroach further on the middle
ground of work and love where activity is shared.

One more illustration of the juxtaposition between incorporation and agency belongs here. Few of the partisans
of incorporation are able to carry on a discussion which
really brings the terms together. Norman O. Brown is an
exception. He speaks with a native clairvoyance as remarkable as Emerson's. When Brown refers to Hegel's "aggres-
sive principle of negativity," much of the matter of this
book is caught in a phrase, and Brown makes his choice
in the very terms of the intellect he loathes. Thought, he
is saying, proceeds by denials and affirmations, involves
negations, real and differencing negations: thought is

genital and bad. What appears to have begun with Emerson has for the moment ended here.

The final stress ought to fall on an acknowledgment that I have only reported what has been imagined, and that the distinction between incorporation and agency is not a basis for an exhaustive account of the American past. But I hope to follow this strand into a later period. Why did industrialism have no imaginative consequences proportionate to the profound changes it worked? Does an inner imperialism account for this, and is its present ascendancy evidence that the cultural historian must look elsewhere for evidence of what appears to be a continuity? Was it not Emerson's man whom Dewey saw seated in the schoolroom?

Appendix

Crossing Brooklyn Ferry

I

Flood-tide below me! I see you face to face!
Clouds of the west—sun there half an hour high—I see you
    also face to face.

Crowds of men and women attired in the usual costumes, how
    curious you are to me!
On the ferry-boats the hundreds and hundreds that cross, re-
    turning home, are more curious to me than you sup-
    pose,
And you that shall cross from shore to shore years hence are
    more to me, and more in my meditations, than you
    might suppose.   5

II

The impalpable sustenance of me from all things at all hours
    of the day,
The simple, compact, well-join'd scheme, myself disintegrated,
    every one disintegrated yet part of the scheme,
The similitudes of the past and those of the future,
The glories strung like beads on my smallest sights and hear-

ings, on the walk in the street and the passage over
    the river,
The current rushing so swiftly and swimming with me far
    away,   10
The others that are to follow me, the ties between me and
    them,
The certainty of others, the life, love, sight, hearing of others.

Others will enter the gates of the ferry and cross from shore
    to shore,
Others will watch the run of the flood-tide,
Others will see the shipping of Manhattan north and west,
    and the heights of Brooklyn to the south and east,   15
Others will see the islands large and small;
Fifty years hence, others will see them as they cross, the sun
    half an hour high,
A hundred years hence, or ever so many hundred years hence,
    others will see them,
Will enjoy the sunset, the pouring-in of the flood-tide, the
    falling-back to the sea of the ebb-tide.

III

It avails not, time nor place—distance avails not,   20
I am with you, you men and women of a generation, or ever
    so many generations hence,
Just as you feel when you look on the river and sky, so I felt,
Just as any of you is one of a living crowd, I was one of a
    crowd,
Just as you are refresh'd by the gladness of the river and the
    bright flow, I was refresh'd,
Just as you stand and lean on the rail, yet hurry with the swift
    current, I stood yet was hurried,   25
Just as you look on the numberless masts of ships and the
    thick-stemm'd pipes of steamboats, I look'd.

I too many and many a time cross'd the river of old,

Watched the Twelfth-month sea-gulls, saw them high in the
    air floating with motionless wings, oscillating their
    bodies,

Saw how the glistening yellow lit up parts of their bodies and
    left the rest in strong shadow,

Saw the slow-wheeling circles and the gradual edging toward
    the south,   30

Saw the reflection of the summer sky in the water,

Had my eyes dazzled by the shimmering track of beams,

Look'd at the fine centrifugal spokes of light round the shape
    of my head in the sunlit water,

Look'd on the haze on the hills southward and south-westward,

Look'd on the vapor as it flew in fleeces tinged with violet,   35

Look'd toward the lower bay to notice the vessels arriving,

Saw their approach, saw aboard those that were near me,

Saw the white sails of schooners and sloops, saw the ships at
    anchor,

The sailors at work in the rigging or out astride the spars,

The round masts, the swinging motion of the hulls, the slender
    serpentine pennants,   40

The large and small steamers in motion, the pilots in their
    pilothouses,

The white wake left by the passage, the quick tremulous
    whirl of the wheels,

The flags of all nations, the falling of them at sunset,

The scallop-edged waves in the twilight, the ladled cups, the
    frolicsome crests and glistening,

The stretch afar growing dimmer and dimmer, the gray walls
    of the granite storehouses by the docks,   45

On the river the shadowy group, the big steam-tug closely
    flank'd on each side by the barges, the hay-boat, the
    belated lighter,

On the neighboring shore the fires from the foundry chimneys
    burning high and glaringly into the night,

Casting their flicker of black contrasted with wild red and
       yellow light over the tops of houses, and down into
       the clefts of streets.

IV

These and all else were to me the same as they are to you,
I loved well those cities, loved well the stately and rapid river,
The men and women I saw were all near to me,
Others the same—others who look back on me because I   50
       look'd forward to them,
(The time will come, though I stop here to-day and to-night.)

V

What is it then between us?
What is the count of the scores or hundreds of years between
       us?   55

Whatever it is, it avails not—distance avails not, and place
       avails not,
I too lived, Brooklyn of ample hills was mine,
I too walk'd the streets of Manhattan island, and bathed in the
       waters around it,
I too felt the curious abrupt questionings stir within me,
In the day among crowds of people sometimes they came upon
       me,   60
In my walks home late at night or as I lay in my bed they came
       upon me,
I too had been struck from the float forever held in solution,
I too had receiv'd identity by my body,
That I was I knew was of my body, and what I should be I
       knew I should be of my body.

VI

It is not upon you alone the dark patches fall, 65
The dark threw its patches down upon me also,
The best I had done seem'd to me blank and suspicious,
My great thoughts as I supposed them, were they not in reality
　　meagre?
Nor is it you alone who know what it is to be evil,
I am he who knew what it was to be evil, 70
I too knitted the old knot of contrariety,
Blabb'd, blush'd, resented, lied, stole, grudg'd,
Had guile, anger, lust, hot wishes I dared not speak,
Was wayward, vain, greedy, shallow, sly, cowardly, malig-
　　nant,
The wolf, the snake, the hog, not wanting in me, 75
The cheating look, the frivolous word, the adulterous wish,
　　not wanting,
Refusals, hates, postponements, meanness, laziness, none of
　　these wanting,
Was one with the rest, the days and haps of the rest,
Was call'd by my nighest name by clear loud voices of young
　　men as they saw me approaching or passing,
Felt their arms on my neck as I stood, or the negligent leaning
　　of their flesh against me as I sat, 80
Saw many I loved in the street or ferry-boat or public assem-
　　bly, yet never told them a word,
Lived the same life with the rest, the same old laughing,
　　gnawing, sleeping,
Play'd the part that still looks back on the actor or actress,
The same old role, the role that is what we make it, as great
　　as we like,
Or as small as we like, or both great and small. 85

VII

Closer yet I approach you,
What thought you have of me now, I had as much of you——I
      laid in my stores in advance,
I consider'd long and seriously of you before you were born.

Who was to know what should come home to me?
Who knows but I am enjoying this?   90
Who knows, for all the distance, but I am as good as looking
      at you now, for all you cannot see me?

VIII

Ah, what can ever be more stately and admirable to me than
      mast-hemm'd Manhattan?
River and sunset and scallop-edg'd waves of flood-tide?
The sea-gulls oscillating their bodies, the hay-boat in the twi-
      light, and the belated lighter?
What gods can exceed these that clasp me by the hand, and
      with voices I love call me promptly and loudly by my
      nighest name as I approach?   95
What is more subtle than this which ties me to the woman or
      man that looks in my face?
Which fuses me into you now, and pours my meaning into
      you?

We understand then do we not?
What I promis'd without mentioning it, have you not ac-
      cepted?
What the study could not teach——what the preaching could
      not accomplish is accomplish'd, is it not?   100

IX

Flow on, river! flow with the flood-tide, and ebb with the ebb-
tide!

Frolic on, crested and scallop-edg'd waves!

Gorgeous clouds of the sunset! drench with your splendor me,
or the men and women generations after me!

Cross from shore to shore, countless crowds of passengers!

Stand up, tall masts of Mannahatta! stand up, beautiful hills
of Brooklyn!   *105*

Throb, baffled and curious brain! throw out questions and answers!

Suspend here and everywhere, eternal float of solution!

Gaze, loving and thirsting eyes, in the house or street or public assembly!

Sound out, voices of young men! loudly and musically call me
by my nighest name!

Live, old life! play the part that looks back on the actor or
actress!   *110*

Play the old role, the role that is great or small according as
one makes it!

Consider, you who peruse me, whether I may not in unknown
ways be looking upon you;

Be firm, rail over the river, to support those who lean idly,
yet haste with the hasting current;

Fly on, sea-birds! fly sideways, or wheel in large circles high
in the air;

Receive the summer sky, you water, and faithfully hold it
till all downcast eyes have time to take it from you! *115*

Diverge, fine spokes of light, from the shape of my head, or
any one's head, in the sunlit water!

Come on, ships from the lower bay! pass up or down, white-
sail'd schooners, sloops, lighters!

Flaunt away, flags of all nations! be duly lower'd at sunset!

Burn high your fires, foundry chimneys! cast black shadows

at nightfall! cast red and yellow light over the tops of
    the houses!
Appearances, now or henceforth, indicate what you are,   120
You necessary film, continue to envelop the soul,
About my body for me, and your body for you, be hung our
    divinest aromas,
Thrive, cities—bring your freight, bring your shows, ample
    and sufficient rivers,
Expand, being than which none else is perhaps more spiritual,
Keep your places, objects than which none else is more lasting.   125

You have waited, you always wait, you dumb, beautiful
    ministers,
We receive you with free sense at last, and are insatiate
    henceforward,
Not you any more shall be able to foil us, or withhold
    yourselves from us,
We use you, and do not cast you aside—we plant you
    permanently within us,
We fathom you not—we love you—there is perfection in you
    also,   130
You furnish your parts toward eternity,
Great or small, you furnish your parts toward the soul.

Notes

Chapter I

The Failure
of the Fathers

1 *The Complete Works of Ralph Waldo Emerson*, 12 vols. (Boston, 1903–4), I, 338. Source cited hereafter as *Works*.

2 A familiar point; in the *Literary History of the United States*, 2 vols. (New York, 1948) it is stated (p. 346) that Emerson, Thoreau, Hawthorne, Melville and Whitman dealt in the "perspective of humanity itself." And H. B. Parkes is more explicit: "And being concerned not with the analysis of a society, but with the most elemental problems of man's place in the universe, some of them [American writers] went more deeply into the human situation than any of their European contemporaries except the Russians, in spite of their lack of breadth and variety. As D. H. Lawrence said, they reached a verge." *The American Experience* (New York, 1947), pp. 186–7.

3 *The Journals of Ralph Waldo Emerson*, 10 vols. (Boston, 1909–14), IV, 16: "There is such an immense background to my nature that I must treat my fellow as Empire treats Empire and God God." Source cited hereafter as *Journals*.

4 Perry Miller: *The Life of the Mind in America from the Revolution to the Civil War* (New York, 1965), "Book One," *passim*.

5 Alexis de Tocqueville: *Democracy in America*, 2 vols., ed. Phillips Bradley (New York, 1954), I, 315–16.

6 *Journals*, IV, 149–50.

7 Ibid., III, 73.

8 Walt Whitman: "Song of Myself," Section 41, Line 1043, in *Leaves of Grass: Comprehensive Reader's Edition*, ed. Harold W. Blodgett and Sculley Bradley (New York, 1965), p. 75.

9 *Journals*, III, 123. The alternative is above or beside the social world: "Our thought is now the community of which you and I and all are members"; *The Letters of Ralph Waldo Emerson*, 6 vols., ed. Ralph Leslie Rusk (New York, 1939), II, 213 (source cited hereafter as *Letters*). See also *Journals*, III, 414.

10 George Santayana: *Character and Opinion in the United States* (New York, 1920), p. 13.

11 George Santayana: *Interpretations of Poetry and Religion* (New York, 1900), p. 176.

12 See *Works*, II, 29: "He learns again what moral vigor is needed to supply the girdle of a superstition."

13 *Journals*, II, 273; Nicolas Berdyaev: *The Beginning and the End* (New York, 1957), p. 135.

14 A. Robert Caponigri: "Brownson and Emerson: Nature and History," *The New England Quarterly*, XVIII (September 1945), 373.

15 *Journals*, II, 310. Emerson uses "idiosyncratic" pejoratively a few pages later (p. 324). The point is that we are persons in our own view, but that to claim or enjoy the status of a "personage" is to blind ourselves to the nature of the uniqueness which alone connects us with the universal. The emphasis is familiar from Boehme to Berdyaev; what concerns me here is Emerson's own use of it.

16 Austin Warren puts him with Montaigne, Pascal, Amiel, and Nietzsche. "He is not primarily a 'maker' either of po-

etry or philosophy but a 'seeker' "; *New England Saints* (Ann Arbor, Mich., 1956), p. 46.

17 Tocqueville: op. cit., II, 11, 82.

18 David H. Fischer: *The Revolution of American Conservatism* (New York, 1965).

19 *Works*, III, 78.

20 Ibid., pp. 80–1.

21 Ibid., I, 73–4.

22 *Journals*, II, 270.

23 William Ellery Channing, in *Christian Examiner*, V (March and April, 1828), 143, 148.

24 Jones Very: "Influence of Christianity and of the Progress of Civilization on Epic Poetry," *Christian Examiner*, XXIV (March, May, and July, 1838), 201–21. "We have thus endeavored to show the inability of the human mind, at the present day, to represent objectively its own action on another mind, and that the power to do this could alone enable the poet to embody in his hero the present development of the heroic character, and give to his poem a universal interest. We rejoice at this inability; it is the high privilege of our age, the greatest proof of the progress of the soul, and of its approach to that state of being where its thought is action, its word power." Note that Emerson's assertion of the incommensurability of one mind's vision with another's is here said to have arisen within history, and that the apocalyptic note is strongly struck. What Emerson had only at *moments* is here represented as an approaching climax in historical time.

25 William Ellery Channing, in *Christian Examiner*, VI (March 1829), 5.

26 William Ellery Channing, in *Christian Examiner*, VII (September 1829), 112.

27 Thomas Carlyle: "Characteristics," *Edinburgh Review*, LIV (1831), 360.

28 *Journals*, V, 380.

29 William Ellery Channing, in *Christian Examiner*, VI (March 1829), 17.

30 Frederick Henry Hedge, in *Christian Examiner*, XIV (March, May, and July, 1833), 119.

31 Andrew Peabody, in *Christian Examiner*, XXVI (March–July, 1839), 77.

32 Orestes Brownson, in *Christian Examiner*, XVIII (March, May, and July, 1835). *An Essay on the Moral Constitution and History of Man* (Edinburgh, 1834), pp. 345–68. (A review.)

33 Francis Bowen, in *Christian Examiner*, XXI (September 1836–January 1837), 374–5.

34 Stephen E. Whicher: *Freedom and Fate: An Inner Life of Ralph Waldo Emerson* (Philadelphia, 1953).

35 Sherman Paul: *Emerson's Angle of Vision* (Cambridge, Mass., 1952).

36 Charles Feidelson, Jr.: *Symbolism and American Literature* (Chicago, 1953). This seems to me the work of one of the ablest minds ever to deal with American literature. But it is almost impossible to read now (eighteen years later) because its isolation of artist and works in a realm of art is so claustral. Almost every issue of importance is refracted into this oddly insular world. But there are no persons with imaginative or emotional commitments in the context Feidelson creates; there is no history save that of the inwardly determined symbolizing process itself. The book is now a rather scary exhibition of the costs of denying history. See, in particular, pp. 98, 123.

37 John Jay Chapman: *Emerson and Other Essays* (New York, 1898); William James: *Memories and Studies* (New York, 1911); John Dewey: *Character and Events* (New York, 1929).

38 Of course, some of the American New Critics started out

with a social commitment to a conservative agrarianism, and the assumption of posts in the academy by many other critics meant that the impulse to come out of time and abandon politics was shared by those who had earlier been radicals as well as by those who had been conservatives.

39 "The Context of Criticism," *The Sewanee Review*, LXIV (Autumn 1956), 651–7. (A review of R. W. B. Lewis' *The American Adam*.)

40 Jonathan Bishop: *Emerson on the Soul* (Cambridge, Mass., 1964). This is the most various, sensitive, and intelligent of all books on Emerson. Bishop sees and states some of the most important elements of the case I have presented, but ends by subduing himself to an atemporal and inhumane critical position.

41 *Works*, I, 111.

42 Ibid., II, 27.

43 *Journals*, III, 377.

44 Ibid., 337–8.

45 See the passage quoted above, p. 30.

46 As Constance Rourke saw; *American Humor* (New York, 1953), p. 134.

47 *Journals*, V, 462–3.

48 Wordsworth referred in *The Prelude* (Book II, Lines 279–81) to the loss of the "props" of his affections—that is, both his parents—and to the wonder that his psychic constitution stood without their aid.

49 Ralph Leslie Rusk: *The Life of Ralph Waldo Emerson* (New York, 1949), p. 261.

50 The notion of "compensation" is an attempt to move ethics within the self—to reassure oneself that all will be well eventually. But its awkwardness for Emerson is obvious; it is a temporal notion, and as such did not fit his widest sense of things.

51 *The Correspondence of Thomas Carlyle and Ralph Waldo*

Emerson, ed. Charles Eliot Norton 2 vols. (Boston, 1884), I, 33.

52 *Journals*, IV, 495.

Chapter II

Hawthorne's Boston

1 *The Centenary Edition of the Works of Nathaniel Haw-thorne*, 5 vols. issued (Columbus, Ohio, 1962–8), III, 103. (All citations from Hawthorne are from this edition, hereafter cited as *Centenary Edition.*)

2 Denis Donoghue: *The Ordinary Universe: Soundings in Modern Literature* (London, 1968).

3 Malcolm Bradbury: "Towards a Poetics of Fiction," *Novel: A Forum on Fiction*, I (Fall 1967), 47.

4 Lionel Trilling: "Our Hawthorne," in *Hawthorne Centenary Essays*, ed. Roy Harvey Pearce (Columbus, Ohio, 1964), pp. 429–58.

5 Ibid., p. 457.

6 Frederick Crews: *The Sins of the Fathers* (New York, 1966).

7 Ibid., p. 251.

8 Ibid., p. 257.

9 Ibid., p. 102.

10 Ibid., p. 106.

11 See Malcolm Cowley: *The Portable Hawthorne* (New York, 1948), p. 18. Cowley's use of "fields of force" carries a similar suggestion about these oppositions, as does this sentence from R. W. B. Lewis: "In *The Scarlet Letter* not only do the individual and the world, the conduct and the

institutions, measure each other: the measurement and its consequences are precisely and centrally what the novel is about"; *The American Adam* (Chicago, 1955), p. 112. Rudolph Von Abele had earlier made a similar point in "The Scarlet Letter: A Reading," *Accent*, XI (Autumn 1951), 211–27 (see especially p. 224).

12 *Centenary Edition*, I, 166.
13 Ibid., p. 127; see also pp. 64, 84, 139, 142, 234, 250, 254.
14 John Thompson: "American Dreamers" (a review of Marius Bewley's *The Eccentric Design*), *The Hudson Review*, XII (Autumn 1959), 440–5.
15 Henry James: *Hawthorne* (Ithaca, N.Y., 1956), p. 90.
16 *Centenary Edition*, I, 48.
17 Ibid., III, 198.
18 Crews: op. cit., pp. 147–8.
19 *Centenary Edition*, I, 222.
20 Crews: op. cit., pp. 147–8.

Chapter III

———

Consciousness and Form
in Whitman

1 *Henry James' Autobiography*, ed. F. W. Dupee (New York, 1956), p. 16.
2 Walt Whitman: "Crossing Brooklyn Ferry," Section 5, Line 62, in *Leaves of Grass: Comprehensive Reader's Edition*, ed. Harold W. Blodgett and Sculley Bradley (New York, 1965), p. 162. (Source cited hereafter as *Comprehensive Edition*.)

3 Claude Lévi-Strauss: *The Savage Mind* (Chicago, 1966). See, particularly, pp. 18–20, 155–60, 266–9.

4 Reuel Denney: "How Americans See Themselves," in *Studies in American Culture*, ed. Joseph Kwiat and Mary C. Turpie (Minneapolis, 1960), p. 23.

5 Norman O. Brown: *Life Against Death: The Psychoanalytical Meaning of History* (Middletown, Conn., 1959), pp. 23–39.

6 I have sketched a treatment of Brooks, Cather and Frost. See "The Critic and Imperial Consciousness," *New Republic*, Vol. 152 (April 17, 1965), pp. 15–17, for Van Wyck Brooks; "Willa Cather: Her Masquerade," *New Republic*, Vol. 153 (November 27, 1965), pp. 28–31; and "Frost's Way: Making the Most of It," *The Nation* (February 6, 1967), 182–4.

7 I have treated the elder Henry James in *The American Henry James* (New Brunswick, N.J., 1957), Chap. III and *passim*. The fullest account of his work is Frederic Harold Young: *The Philosophy of Henry James, Sr.* (New York, 1951), which has a good bibliography of writings by and about him. A selection of his letters may be found in Ralph Barton Perry: *The Thought and Character of William James*, 2 vols. (Boston, 1935), and in F. O. Matthiessen: *The James Family* (New York, 1947). Like Blake, he is easily distorted when quoted out of context, and he has not yet found his Northrop Frye. James Sr.'s *Substance and Shadow* (Boston, 1863), which deals more explicitly than his other works with contemporary philosophy, is the best book to start with.

8 Henry James, Sr.: *Substance and Shadow* (Boston, 1863), p. 323.

9 Ibid., pp. 210–11.

10 Ibid., p. 209.

11 Ibid., p. 405.

12 See Fredrick Schyberg: *Whitman* (New York, 1951) and

Roger Asselineau: *The Evolution of Walt Whitman*, 2 vols. (Cambridge, Mass., 1960).

13 Harold Bloom: *Blake's Apocalypse: A Study in Poetic Argument* (Garden City, N.Y., 1963).

14 "Song of Myself," Section 8, Line 155, in *Comprehensive Edition*, p. 36.

15 "Song of Myself," Section 31, Line 670, ibid., p. 59.

16 "Sailing to Byzantium," in *The Collected Poems of W. B. Yeats* (New York, 1933), p. 191.

17 *The Collected Tales of E. M. Forster* (New York, 1947), pp. 128–30.

18 "Whitman," in *Studies in Classic American Literature* (New York, 1923); see, particularly, pp. 249–53.

19 "Song of Myself," Section 32, Line 684, in *Comprehensive Edition*, p. 60.

20 "Song of Myself," Section 13, Line 244, ibid., p. 40.

21 R. M. Rilke: "The Eighth Elegy," in *Duino Elegies* (bilingual edn.), trans. J. B. Leishman and Stephen Spender (New York, 1939), pp. 66–71.

22 "A Song of Joys," Line 198, in *Comprehensive Edition*, p. 181.

23 "A Song of Joys," Line 141, ibid., p. 182.

24 Frank Kermode: *Romantic Image* (London, 1957), p. 161.

25 William Wordsworth: "Ode: Intimations of Immortality from Recollections of Early Childhood," Line 51.

26 "Among School Children," in *The Collected Poems of W. B. Yeats*, p. 214.

27 "A Song for Occupations," Section 3, Line 59, in *Comprehensive Edition*, p. 214.

28 Northrop Frye: *Fearful Symmetry* (Boston, 1962), p. 420.

29 Frank Kermode: *The Sense of an Ending* (New York, 1967), p. 41.

30 Letter to George and Georgiana Keats (Friday, March

19, 1819), in *The Complete Poetical Works and Letters of John Keats*, ed. Horace E. Scudder (Cambridge, Mass., 1899), p. 363.

31 See Section 29 of "Song of Myself," in *Comprehensive Edition*, p. 58.

Chapter IV

The World in the Body

1 William Troy: "The Altar of Henry James" (1943), in *The Question of Henry James*, ed. F. W. Dupee (New York, 1945), p. 110.

2 See Preface (1855), Lines 581–603 and 479 *ff.*; "Song of Myself," Section 21; and "Crossing Brooklyn Ferry," Sections 1 and 2. All in Walt Whitman: *Leaves of Grass: Comprehensive Reader's Edition*, ed. Harold W. Blodgett and Sculley Bradley (New York, 1965). (Source hereafter cited as *Comprehensive Edition*.)

3 For the quotation in full, see p. 176.

4 John Kinnaird: "Leaves of Grass and the American Paradox," in *Whitman: A Collection of Critical Essays*, ed. Roy Harvey Pearce (Englewood, N.J., 1962), pp. 24–36. (Kinnaird's essay was first published as "Whitman: The Paradox of Identity," *Partisan Review*, XXV [Summer 1958], 380–405.)

5 Ibid., p. 29.

6 Leslie Fiedler: "Images of Walt Whitman," in *Leaves of Grass One Hundred Years After*, ed. Milton Hindus (Stanford, Cal, 1955), pp. 55–73.

7 Paul Fussell: "Whitman's Curious Warble," in *The Pres-*

ence of Walt Whitman, ed. R. W. B. Lewis (New York, 1962), p. 51.

8 See Kinnaird's essay in *Whitman: A Collection of Critical Essays*, p. 34. "The irony of the 'untranslatable' mystery begins to disappear in the very year of publication, for in the performance of 1856 Whitman has already begun to lose the delicate balance of his paradox. The first *Leaves of Grass*, the actual book, seems to have served Whitman as a kind of mirror, in which the *persona*, having acquired objective reality, saw itself for the first time; and from that moment, as it were, Whitman's love was less for her democratic mystery than for its American image."

9 See "Spontaneous Me," Line 37, in *Comprehensive Edition*, p. 105, and note the context in which it occurs.

10 R. M. Rilke: "The Second Elegy," in *Duino Elegies* (bilingual edn.), trans. J. B. Leishman and Stephen Spender (New York, 1939), p. 28.

11 Géza Róheim: *The Gates of the Dream* (New York, 1952).

12. See also the opening lines of Section 40, "Song of Myself," in *Comprehensive Edition*, p. 73.

13 The association of light with flood that I have noted as recurrent above might have come about for Whitman if he knew the use of "float" in the singular for a row of footlights. Harold Blodgett and Sculley Bradley apparently assume that he did; *Comprehensive Edition*, pp. 152–3 *n*. But the *O.E.D.* does not record the use in the singular before 1862.

"Light and flood" usually refers to the light of vision associated with liquid in a context of generation. For example, note (from "I Sing the Body Electric," in *Comprehensive Edition*, p. 83):

Do you suppose you have a right to a good sight, and
he or she has no right to a sight?

> *Do you think matter has cohered together from its*
> *diffuse float, and the soil is on the surface, and*
> *water runs and vegetation sprouts,*
> *For you only, and not for him and her?*

14 "Song of Myself," Section 22, in *Comprehensive Edition*, p. 49.

15 Note the 1855 version of Section 8 of "The Sleepers," (in *Leaves of Grass* [New York, 1855]):

> *Not you will yield forth the dawn again more surely*
> *than you will yield forth me again,*
> *Not the womb yields the babe in its time more surely*
> *than I shall be yielded from you in my time.*

16 A different emphasis on the significance of this kind of emotional commitment in the context of a discussion of society is to be found in Herbert Marcuse: *Eros and Civilization* (New York, 1955), pp. 45 *ff*. Marcuse also quotes (p. 147) a significant sonnet by Rilke, which involves the notion of incorporating the world.

17 George Santayana: *Interpretations of Poetry and Religion* (New York, 1900), Chap. VII ("The Poetry of Barbarism").

18 See John Jay Chapman: "Walt Whitman," in *Emerson and Other Essays* (New York, 1898).

19 See "Spontaneous Me," Line 22, and the use of the word "undulating" in "I Sing the Body Electric," Line 62. Both in *Comprehensive Edition*, pp. 103–5 and 93–101, respectively.

20 See Sigmund Freud: "Psychoanalytic Notes upon an Autobiographical Account of a Case of Paranoia (Dementia Paranoides)" (1911), in *Collected Papers*, 24 vols., authorized trans. by Alix and James Strachey (New York, 1959), III, 390–470.

21 Géza Róheim: *Psychoanalysis and Anthropology* (New York, 1950), p. 35.

22 "The Emperor of Ice-Cream," in *The Collected Poems of Wallace Stevens* (New York, 1954), p. 64. We can't avoid paradox on this point. See Section 7 of Whitman's "To Think of Time" (*Comprehensive Edition*, p. 438), in which the use of the transient to constitute the permanent —that planted "within us"—is baldly asserted.

Chapter V

The Golden Bowl as a Cultural Artifact

1 T. S. Eliot: "On Henry James" (1918), in *The Question of Henry James*, ed. F. W. Dupee (New York, 1945), p. 110.

2 William Troy: "The Altar of Henry James" (1943), in ibid., p. 272.

3 It should be noted that in his first volume, *Henry James: The Untried Years, 1843–1870* (Philadelphia and New York, 1953), Professor Edel suggests, in a narrower context than I employ, an antithesis between James' personal passivity and his activity as artist. See pp. 65–6.

4 Francis Fergusson: "The Golden Bowl Revisited," in *The Human Image in Dramatic Literature* (New York, 1957), p. 185.

5 Edith Wharton: *A Backward Glance* (New York, 1964), p. 178.

6 The dialogue "Daniel Deronda: A Conversation" has been widely reprinted. It is available in *A Century of George*

Eliot Criticism, ed. Gordon S. Haight (Boston, 1965), pp. 97–112.

7 The novelist's distinction between the two loves is succinctly put in *The Tragic Muse* (New York edn., 1907–17), p. 148: "If the affection that isolates and simplifies its object may be distinguished from the affection that seeks communications and contacts for it, Julia Dallow's was quite of the encircling, not to say the narrowing sort." Cf. *The Journals of Ralph Waldo Emerson*, 10 vols. (Boston, 1909–14), V, 552: "He must emanate; he must give all he takes, nor desire to appropriate and to stand still."

8 Henry James: *The Golden Bowl* (Dell paperback, New York, 1963), p. 72. (The notes on *The Golden Bowl* that follow relate to this edition.)

9 Ibid., p. 26.

10 Quentin Anderson: *The American Henry James* (New Brunswick, N.J., 1957), Chap. X ("The Golden Bowl").

11 *The Golden Bowl*, p. 207.

12 Ibid., pp. 105–6.

13 Henry James: *A Small Boy and Others* (New York, 1913), pp. 345–9.

14 This and the preceding quotations are to be found in Henry James: "The Question of Our Speech" and "The Lesson of Balzac," in *Two Lectures* (Cambridge, Mass., 1905), pp. 10, 24, 25, and 43.

15 *The Golden Bowl*, p. 496.

16 Ibid., p. 393.

17 Ibid., p. 394.

18 The Prince offers Adam "a contact that, beguilingly, almost confoundingly, was a contact but with practically yielding lines and curved surfaces"; *The Golden Bowl*, p. 103. The "golden drops" of Adam's insights "gathered in no concavity"; p. 104.

19 Ibid., p. 511.

20 Ibid., p. 243.

21 See the reference to the "two loves," note 7 above.

22 *The Golden Bowl*, p. 505.

23 Oscar Cargill in "Mr. James' Aesthetic Mr. Nash," *Nineteenth-Century Fiction*, XII (December 1957), 177–87, and in "Gabriel Nash—Somewhat Less than Angel?", *Nineteenth-Century Fiction*, XIV (December 1959), 231–9, appears to argue that Gabriel Nash cannot be regarded as a voice for the elder James's views—even *says* he has done so in the second of these pieces—but never actually gets around to it. Instead, he offers his own candidate, Oscar Wilde—which appears to trivialize the issues of the novel.

24 Henry James: *Notes of a Son and Brother* (New York, 1914), p. 225.

25 *The Golden Bowl*, p. 105.

26 See a letter to T. S. Perry, November 1863: "We are certainly born to believe. The Truth was certainly made to be believed. Life is a prolonged reconciliation of these two facts. As long as we squint at the Truth instead of looking straight at it—i.e. as long as we are prejudiced instead of fair, so long we are miserable sinners. But it seems to me that this fatal obliquity of vision inheres not wholly in any individual but is some indefinable property in the social atmosphere.—When by some concerted movement of humanity the air is purified then the film will fall from our eyes and . . . we shall gaze undazzled at the sun." "Letters from the Jameses," in Virginia Harlow: *Thomas Sergeant Perry: A Biography* (Durham, N.C., 1950), pp. 270–1. The notion of the "turn of the inward wheel," his father's sense of an apocalyptic resolution of human affairs, was here employed to represent his own sense of things by the youngster of twenty.

27 See R. P. Blackmur's first introduction to *The Golden Bowl* (New York, 1952), p. vii.

28 *The Journals of Ralph Waldo Emerson*, 10 vols. (Boston, 1909–14), II, 310.
29 R. P. Blackmur's introduction to *The Golden Bowl*, p. ix.
30 Ibid., p. x.
31 Ibid., p. xxi.
32 *The Golden Bowl* (New York, 1963), p. 9.

Chapter VI

Coming Out of Culture

1 Henry James: *Selected Short Stories*, ed. Quentin Anderson (New York, 1950). See, particularly, the Introduction, pp. xvii–xviii.
2 Tom Wolfe: *The Electric Kool-Aid Acid Test* (New York, 1968).
3 The case for including Santayana and Shaw here has been convincingly made in two recent Columbia University dissertations in English by Lois Hughson and Daniel A. Dervin.
4 *The Expense of Vision: Essays on the Craft of Henry James* (Princeton, 1964).
5 *The Complete Works of Ralph Waldo Emerson*, 12 vols. (Boston, 1903–14), III, 60. Source cited hereafter as *Works*.
6 Henry James: *The Golden Bowl* (Dell paperback, New York, 1963), p. 85.
7 Walt Whitman: "Song of Myself," Section 44, in *Leaves of Grass: Comprehensive Reader's Edition*, ed. Harold W. Blodgett and Sculley Bradley (New York, 1965), p. 80.

8 Lionel Trilling: "Hawthorne in Our Time," in *Beyond Culture* (New York, 1965), pp. 179–208.

9 Herbert Marcuse: *One-Dimensional Man* (Boston, 1964).

10 *The Blithedale Romance*, in *The Centenary Edition of the Works of Nathaniel Hawthorne*, 5 vols. issued (Columbus, Ohio, 1962–8), III, 70–1.

11 Ralph Waldo Emerson: *Natural History of Intellect*, in *Works*, XII, p. 62.

12 See Perry Miller: *Nature's Nation* (Cambridge, Mass., 1967).

13 Richard Hofstadter: *Anti-intellectualism in American Life* (New York, 1962), p. 48.

14 Perry Miller: *The Life of the Mind in America from the Revolution to the Civil War* (New York, 1965).

15 Tocqueville analyzed the differences between an "aristocratic" age, in which the institutions link men closely with their fellows and involve them with something outside themselves, and a democracy, which "makes men forget their ancestors" and "isolates them from their contemporaries" and lets them "imagine their whole destiny is in their own hands." His observation of America in the 1830's led him to the conclusion: "Each man is forever thrown back on himself alone, and there is a danger he may be shut up in the solitude of his own heart." See *Democracy in America*, ed. J. P. Mayer (New York, 1969), p. 508.

16 Fred Somkin: *Unquiet Eagle: Memory and Desire in the Idea of American Freedom, 1815–1860* (Ithaca, N.Y., 1967).

17 David H. Fischer: *The Revolution of American Conservatism* (New York, 1965).

18 James West: *Plainville, U.S.A.* (New York, 1945).

19 For Ginsberg's sense of the tie between Whitman and himself on the question of divided social roles, see Hunter S.

Thompson: *Hell's Angels* (Penguin Books, 1967), pp. 258–64. The phrase "harmless emptiness" occurs on p. 263.

20 Lawrence's *Studies* may be found conveniently in *The Shock of Recognition*, ed. Edmund Wilson (New York, 1955). See pp. 964, 1063–4, and 1065–6 for these quotations.

Index

QUENTIN ANDERSON directs the graduate study of American literature at Columbia University, and was for some years head of the English Department of Columbia College. He is the author of *The American Henry James*.

VINTAGE POLITICAL SCIENCE
AND SOCIAL CRITICISM

VINTAGE CRITICISM,
LITERATURE, MUSIC, AND ART

VINTAGE BIOGRAPHY AND AUTOBIOGRAPHY

VINTAGE HISTORY—AMERICAN